I MUST HAVE WANDERED

INTRODUCTION

This is my story of an infant who was brought into a family with roots and branches that did not belong to her. The roots of her adoptive family intertwined with her persistent fibers of self, often in confusing ways. The couple thought she came to them as a *tabula rasa*, a blank slate, and they hoped to etch their likeness, to imprint their heritage, on her. They nurtured, protected, and shaped her—these strangers—yet she remained unchanged: strong, determined, rebellious, and questioning.

This is my story of a girl's and then a woman's struggle to restore her identity. Some of my efforts were rewarded and some not. In South Carolina, my birth state, adoptees' vital records have been sealed from our viewing and possession since 1964 when I was twelve. My adoptive parents likely weren't aware of that sealing, nor would they have objected had they known. They had, after all, been told by the agency that next to nothing was known about my birth mother and her family, and they never questioned the authority of the church. I am a perpetual child in the view of church and state with no agency in a law that marginalizes me and strips me of a right to my identification. What is more, the agency, purported to be built on charity, is a willing participant in the law that falsified church and state documents and denies me my original birth records.

My adoptee story was made complex by military life. As a subject of primal separation, my family transience and separations felt overbearing. I coped and asserted myself without a clear path and continuous connections that neighborhood, school, lifelong friends, and extended family can provide. Still, I reaped the benefits of an enlarged experience brought by Air Force life.

My parents' duty was to protect and save me from what might have been. From the harms of abandonment. From my birth mother's original sin. From the limbo of lost babies in the infant home. My story is told through old letters my adoptive parents wrote, baby book notes, myriad photos, and my memories. It's a story of the recovery of pieces scattered and strewn like breadcrumbs when my natural mother gave me up to strangers, and the pieces I've gathered to recover myself. My life stories resided in fable until my truth was revealed—expanded by discovery.

This is a work of creative nonfiction; an epistolary memoir. It is a collage of letters, fragments, vignettes, lyric prose, and narrative. Most names are kept; a few are changed to protect privacy. The memory of dialogue is notoriously inadequate and flawed, and I attempt to portray conversations in their context. My youngest memories of places and events are based on photos augmented by firsthand family descriptions and stories. I sometimes write from the perspective of perhaps. My truths are intact, and I've researched facts to the best of my ability. Adoptee Resources and reading appear at the end of the book.

I Must Have Wandered

An Adopted Air Force Daughter Recalls

MARY ELLEN GAMBUTTI

LUMINARE PRESS

WWW.LUMINAREPRESS.COM

Printed in the United States of America

Luminare Press
442 Charnelton St.
Eugene, OR 97401
www.luminarepress.com

LCCN: 2022903565
ISBN: 978-1-64388-862-0

To Phil

CONTENTS

PART TWENTY

PART TWENTY-ONE

ADVANCE PRAISE

Mary Ellen Gambutti's memoir, *I Must Have Wandered: An Adopted Air Force Daughter Recalls,* is not just another adoption search memoir. This quest memoir is a hybrid collection of letters, narrative, lyric essays, and prose poetry. She weaves the elements of her fascinating and complex history together like the threads in a fine tapestry. Gambutti's story is masterfully told and well executed. Hers is an exciting new voice making itself heard among a growing throng of female adoption writers.

> —*Julie Ryan McGue, author of Twice a Daughter:*
> *A Search for Identity, Family, and Belonging*

I Must Have Wandered is a lyrical and descriptive glimpse into the coming-of-age experiences of an adopted military daughter in the 1950s and 1960s and her emergence into young adulthood as she explores issues with attachment, trust, identity, and direction. This is a well-written must read for baby boomer/baby scoop-era adoptees. The complexity of the adoptee's search for place and self in this world is universal, powerful, and effectively explained.

> —*Paige Adams Strickland, author of Akin to the Truth: A*
> *Memoir of Adoption and Identity and After the Truth*

I Must Have Wandered: An Adopted Air Force Daughter Recalls is unique in that it is a sort of epistolary memoir, using correspondence, documents, articles, and vignettes to tell the true story of adoption loss, trauma, and reckoning. Part transcription, part poetry, and part elegy, Mary Ellen's story is beautifully presented like a kaleidoscope, with different moving parts, simultaneously shaping and being shaped by memory and the process of healing.

As a child of a career military father, the constant moving only contributed to Mary Ellen's feelings of being "unrooted," and her lack of ability to form deep attachments with family and friends only fueled her need for connection and truth later in life. Her search for her identity and biological family over twenty years led to more pain and confusion, but in Mary Ellen's own words, her "efforts were rewarded." She was able to identify and find her biological mother and several half siblings and was, through this journey, transformed "in heart and spirit." Mary Ellen grapples with the universal issues of human longing while praising the unexpected beauty to be found in the wake of grief and sorrow. Her journey into the unknown is brave and exemplary. We can all find pieces of our struggles and joys reflected in Mary Ellen's story—especially those of us touched by adoption.

—*Laureen Pittman, author of The Lies That Bind: An Adoptee's Journey through Rejection, Redirection, DNA, and Discovery*

The myth of the perfectly lovely people who choose adoption is laid bare in Mary Ellen Gambutti's memoir, *I Must Have Wandered*. As if growing up with a sad and withholding mother isn't damaging enough, her ever-absent Air Force father is revealed to have been the former head of the Los Angeles office of the CIA. Gambutti's journey of discovery adds much to the canon of American adoption.

—Rayne Wolfe, author of Toxic Mom Toolkit,
former The New York Times regional staff writer, and
former columnist ("What Works") at San Francisco
Chronicle and The Seattle Times.

I loved this book on so many levels. Mary Ellen expresses her feelings about her adoption with vivid sensory detail. I felt so much empathy, having also grown up in an Air Force family—my dad was a lieutenant colonel and navigator and always spoke to my mother and my siblings about the need for us to observe proper protocol. It was, apparently, important that he maintained control of his family or it would be a reflection of his competence. I grew up in that structured lifestyle, always trying to project a "normal family" image, instead of the truly dysfunctional family we were.

Thus, when I became pregnant my first semester of college, my mother insisted if I ever brought the baby home, Dad would be court-martialed—a concern which I still can't imagine was true. I was totally taken back to my story while reading Mary Ellen's.

—Carol Chandler, Air Force Brat/Birthmother

In Mary Ellen Gambutti's deeply personal memoir, *I Must Have Wandered: An Adopted Air Force Daughter Recalls,* the author yearns to become whole in a life fragmented and uprooted. Propelled by questions like *who am I?* and *where do I belong?* she works diligently to understand herself and her place in the world, but in her adoptive family, she finds neither identity nor belonging.

Though she tries endlessly to please them, her adoptive parents' eyes do not mirror to her, who she is. They offer love on the condition that she meet standards rooted in their unfathomable needs for control and authority. She reacts from an innate refusal to accept the conditions of their relationship. Feeling it her birthright, she has a deep longing for the unconditional love that the people she has been entrusted to are incapable of giving. Gambutti's quest for identity and belonging unfolds like a mystery as she tracks down and investigates clues that help her to understand her origins and fulfill her hopes to find the others in whose eyes she does see herself reflected.

—*Basha Krasnoff, writer, researcher, and editor of six print publications and the online literary journal, Portland Metrozine*

Mary Ellen Gambutti

FOREWORD

What an honor it is to welcome you to this book! Adoption memoirs are an important genre that doesn't get enough attention. We need adoption memoirs; we need more adoption memoirs. We need multiple stories for many reasons. Adoption is multilayered. Popular culture is almost obsessed with the "orphan" story, from Harry Potter to Luke Skywalker to Moses. Nearly every Disney movie includes the theme of early parental separation, yet the stories all of us know are often idealized and simplified, while the truth of adoption is generally complicated, confusing, and messy.

As a culture, we need to confront and dismantle the oversimplified popular understanding of adoption. There is more beauty in the love of sitting in truth with someone than all the unicorns and rainbows promoted through the popular narrative. The truth can set us all free to have more realistic expectations, more compassion, more curiosity, less certainty, and ultimately more connection.

My passion as a therapist who specialized in adoption for more than fifteen years has evolved to focus on helping to inform other therapists through consultation and training. Adoptees are four times more likely to attempt suicide, so the stakes are high if therapists are not adoption informed. Sadly, we are provided almost no education on the impacts of adoption in our training programs. Worse, many times, when adoption is addressed by professors or brought up by students, inaccurate popular culture narratives are promoted, often harming the adoptees in the room. It is no wonder that therapy has been more harmful than helpful for many in the adoption constellation: adoptees, birth parents, and adoptive parents.

Adoption memoirs are an important part of the ongoing development of adoption competency for those who want to work with members of the adoption constellation. Even a caseload full of adoption cannot expose us to the full variety of adoptive experiences impacted by different generations, laws, cultures, etc., or provide us with insight into the variety of interpretations of each experience that can be made by each individual. As Mary Ellen shares her story, you will read the impact of the military on her adoptive family, how that impacted her experiences, and how she processed the layers of her adoption. Loss is a core theme that weaves through adoption experiences, and it was exacerbated for Mary Ellen due to the transitory nature of her father's military career. If her parents had handled those transitions with more awareness of her loss—and how much more powerful it was for her as a young child and adoptee—how might her relationship to grief and loss have been different? How might her relationship with her parents have been different?

We need to read adoption memoirs to understand the depth and complexity of the core adoption themes beyond the simple words. The common core themes in adoption are 1) loss/grief, 2) rejection/abandonment/betrayal, 3) guilt/shame, 4) identity, 5) intimacy, 6) control, and 7) fear. These can be experienced by all members of the adoption constellation, although they may play out in different ways for different individuals.

One thing I appreciate about this book is how Mary Ellen shares from the baby's perspective, even if it is written as a perhaps or wonderings. I often try to help adult adoptees, parents, and therapists to consider the infant's perspective and interpretation of the events that impacted them and helped form their implicit memories. What might have been different for the infant left in a hospital for multiple days or the infant placed into foster care, experiencing multiple separations? We know that infants are primed in utero to seek and attach to the biological mother. We know that early parental separation is a trauma. We know that infants can experience fear before birth and that the absence of or separation from a caretaker creates survival fears. Adoption policies and procedures have largely been set from the adult perspective. As you read this book, note how Mary Ellen interprets the words in the letters she includes and how that is different from how the adults in her story may have interpreted those letters.

All those who love and support members of the adoption constellation need adoption memoirs, because our relationships do not expose us to the depth of the adoption experience. You may read things that don't seem to line up with the person that you know. Perhaps it is different for the person in your life, or perhaps they are not sharing the variations, complexity, and depth of their thoughts, feelings, and experiences. The line between privacy and secrecy in adoption can be fraught. There could be very good reasons why you are not privy to details even when it comes to close friends and family members, or there could be very bad reasons for why details have not been shared. Is it about control or fear or privacy and protection? Consider why they may not be sharing everything with you. How might you express more curiosity, compassion, and openness to the hard truths of adoption? Perhaps you will start by letting them know that you read this book. Perhaps you could ask them to recommend another adoption memoir for you to read.

Lastly, I believe adoption memoirs are important for members of the adoption constellation in providing an opportunity to discover one's own personal ambiguous thoughts and feelings crystallized in another's words. Gathering these phrases and stories can be a way for us to come out of the fog of the false narrative about adoption. I hope as you read that you will find both truths and perhaps your own experience crystalized in Mary Ellen's words.

—*Brooke Randolph, LMHC, therapist, author, speaker, and trainer specializing in adoption and Brainspotting.*

Part One

PROLOGUE

Ties Unbound

On a bitterly cold Pennsylvania day, January 2014, I'm alone in my adoptive mother's bedroom, preparing for her move to an assisted living center. Loose photos and family albums lie on this double bed with its carved pineapple finials. Many of these photos were left behind by her mother, and they, the bed, and its matched, mirrored mahogany bureau—photos scattered across its surface—are now hers. Here is my baby book and framed portraits of me, testaments to new parents' devotion. I juggle all these memories with some of my own.

My nana tucked her photos in scrapbooks where the mucilage of memories has kept them in the safety of black corners. When was the last time they saw daylight? Bundles wrapped in rubber bands, stuffed into shoeboxes; frilly brag books and framed images of nieces and nephews, only a few of whom I've met. Crinkle-edged black-and-whites and faded 1960s color shots from pre-digital years are in my hands.

Who are these people? I recognize the faces of some who have crossed my plane in tangent. We share no heritage, and

I ache for such a bond. As I turn the coarse, corn-colored album leaves, searching captioned names and places, I'm aware that like me, these folks have lived ordinary lives. They were never mine, yet I assume the memory of my adoptive ancestry. *How to solve the quandary that I hold in my hands?*

Angel Child

The couple invited their pastor to a modest Sunday dinner in their tiny Sumter, South Carolina, apartment on East Liberty Street, the same street as St. Anne's Catholic Church. Perhaps Agnes served pot roast and a dessert of angel food cake and tea. She would repeat the story through my childhood about the occasion, marking it as the time Father Bayard introduced her and Al to adoption. The essence of the story follows:

The priest queried the couple, "How is it you've been married five years and have no children?" Al shyly related the story of his life-threatening illness and surgeries in 1935–1936 as the cause of their inability to conceive.

"Well then, you must adopt a child! I can connect you with the right people. Many babies are waiting to be loved by good people such as you."

And so, they decided to embark on the journey to adopt. It was the best alternative to having a natural child in the mind of the obliging priest. This Catholic son and daughter would become parents.

The Hopeful Parents

Agnes was born of Julia Ballas Tokar on a small farm in Three Springs, Pennsylvania, on August 10, 1922. When the mine that employed her father, Michael, closed, he moved his family to New York City: first to the Lower East Side, then to the West Village, and later to St. Paul the Apostle Parish on West Fifty-Ninth Street. Agnes finished grade school at St. Paul's and attended Jean the Baptist all-girls high school.

In 1941, Agnes entered a two-year nursing program at St. Vincent's Hospital in Greenwich Village, and went on to receive a bachelor of science degree in public health nursing at St. John's University. She joined the Brooklyn Visiting Nurse Association and commuted from her parents' apartment on West Fifty-Eighth Street.

Al was born in March 1921, the sixth and youngest child of a first-generation Irish couple, Patrick and Ellen Mary, who lived in the heart of New York City. His mother was forty-three years old at the time of his birth. His parents owned and operated a tavern in the city. He attended St. John the Baptist grade school, and when his family moved to St. Paul the Apostle Parish in 1934, he finished grammar school there. Al and Agnes met through mutual friends at church.

In September 1935, Al entered the Paulist Fathers Junior Seminary. Agnes was well-acquainted with him and recorded details of their friendship in her diary. In November 1935, he had an attack of appendicitis with complications that kept him hospitalized or convalescing at home until September 1936. He resumed study for the priesthood at the Paulist Brothers Junior Seminary in Baltimore but withdrew in 1941 to test his vocation. Around this time, he and Agnes began to talk about marriage. He returned to his parents' home while working as a clerical apprentice for General Motors Acceptance Corporation (GMAC). His father died at sixty-five in April 1942. In August 1942, Al and Agnes were engaged.

He enlisted in the US Army Air Corps in September 1942 and served in Calcutta, India, as a photo technician and camera repairman. He was discharged on February 9, 1946, as a staff sergeant and returned to his mother's apartment and GMAC. He entered night school at St. John's University School of Business Administration. A month after his military discharge, his mother died of a heart attack. He and Agnes married on August 10, 1946, in St. Paul the Apostle Church.

In March 1948, Al was commissioned as a second lieutenant in the Air Force Reserves as an aerial photographic officer. He was recalled to active duty with the Air Force in October 1950 and assigned duties as an assistant photo officer and adjutant of a photo squadron. In April 1951, the squadron was transferred to Shaw Air Force Base, South Carolina. He rented an apartment in Sumter, and in June 1951, Agnes resigned her position in public health nursing and joined him. He was thirty-one, and she was thirty.

Letters of Reference

Many letters were exchanged through the adoption process; references from clergy, including their New York City church associates, and this one from Al's commanding officer:

363d Reconnaissance Technical Squadron
Shaw Air Force Base, South Carolina
7 November 1951
To Whom It May Concern:

It has been brought to my attention that Lieutenant and Mrs. Aloysius A. Caffrey intend to adopt a child. As Lieutenant Caffrey's immediate commanding offi-

cer, I have had an excellent opportunity to observe his habits, manners and character during the past year, and I feel my observations may prove valuable in evaluating Lieutenant Caffrey's desirability as a parent.

Lieutenant Caffrey has served as my adjutant since October 19, 1950. He has performed his duties during this period in a superior manner, his devotion to duty has been outstanding, and I can honestly state that he is one of the most conscientious men I have ever had the pleasure of being associated with. Lieutenant Caffrey has demonstrated to me a high degree of intelligence, unquestioned dependability, mature judgment and sincerity. He is most certainly a credit to the uniform he wears.

I might further state that Lieutenant Caffrey is well liked by his fellow officers. He has a pleasant personality, gets along well with everyone, and treats his fellow human beings with respect. His personal behavior has been unquestioned, and his moral character is outstanding. Although Lieutenant Caffrey and I are of different religious denominations, I know him to be a man of deep religious convictions and belief.

In the past year I have also had the pleasure of meeting and knowing Mrs. Caffrey. Like her husband, she is a fine person, and one whom I feel is well qualified in every respect to assume the responsibilities of parenthood.

Concluding, I would like to make this statement. I know of no couple of my acquaintance who I would consider more deserving or qualified for parenthood through adoption. I feel so strongly that Lieutenant and Mrs. Caffrey would make good parents, that I would go so far as to say that I would not hesitate *giving them my own daughter to raise if I was forced to do so by some unforeseen tragedy.*

If I can be of any further assistance in furnishing information on Lieutenant Caffrey, I would be pleased to do so. Your correspondence will receive my prompt attention.

Sincerely yours,
Samuel A. Custer, Major USAF
Commanding

November 5, 1951
Mr. Austin Gordon
Columbus Avenue between 59th and 60th St.
New York City, New York
Dear Mr. Gordon,

My wife and I are planning on adopting a child, and we need letters from reputable people to the effect that we are practicing Catholics and worthy to be parents of a child. Since you have known my wife and me for several years, I would appreciate a letter of recommendation from you addressed "To whom it may concern." You can mail the letter of recommendation to Reverend Father Nicholas Bayard, Saint Anne's Roman Catholic Church, Sumter, South Carolina.

I would appreciate your giving this your prompt attention, because it is our hope that we may have a child before Christmas.

Sincerely yours,
Aloysius A. Caffrey, 2nd Lt. USAF

This letter is undated; the postmarked envelope is missing.

Reverend Father Thomas McMahon
Church of St. Paul the Apostle
415 West 59th Street
New York City, New York
Dear Father McMahon,

My wife and I are in the process of adopting a child, and the children's home requires a letter from our pastor recommending us as good practicing Catholics. Since I still consider St. Paul the Apostle parish as my home parish, I would appreciate a letter from you to this effect. Since you are constantly meeting people and I may not be too familiar to you, you may remember me better as one of the ushers in the church, and as an ex-member of the Juniorate in Baltimore. Father Joseph Hayes was one of my roommates in Baltimore, and he also knows my wife, Agnes. Father Hayes may have a good word for me.

I have lived in St. Paul's parish since 1934, except for the years during the war when I was in the Air Force. I hope someday to return to St. Paul's when world conditions take a turn for the better, and I once again become a civilian.

A prompt reply from you will be greatly appreciated, and may enable us to have our child before the Christmas holiday. Your letter may be sent to Rev. Father Nicholas Bayard, St. Anne's Roman Catholic Church, Sumter, South Carolina.

Respectfully yours,
Aloysius A. Caffrey, 2nd Lt. USAF

November 8, 1951

Church of St. Paul the Apostle
Paulist Fathers
415 West 59th Street
New York, 19 N.Y.

Lieut. Aloysius A. Caffrey
363 Recon. Tech Squadron
Shaw Air Force Base,
South Carolina

Dear Al,

I received your letter this morning. I am happy to tell you that I have written to Father Bayard giving you the recommendation you desire. You and your wife are to be commended for this wonderful gesture.

> *With every best wish, I am,*
> *Sincerely yours in Christ,*
> *Thomas G. McMahon, C.S.P., Pastor*

(Handwritten by Agnes)

Very Rev. Father Maurice Shean
The Oratory
Rock Hill, South Carolina
Dec. 8, 1951
Dear Father Shean,

Father Nicholas Bayard of St. Anne's parish, Sumter, South Carolina, suggested that we write to you and request an appointment with you regarding the adoption of a child for which we have made an application through Father Bayard. Since my husband is in service, and it is difficult for him to be absent from his duty during the week, I would greatly appreciate it if you could arrange for us to visit you on Sunday afternoon, December 16, 1951, at any hour that is convenient to you. We will keep the day open and await your answer. If you cannot arrange a meeting with us on December 16, we would greatly appreciate your letting us know what Sunday would be possible for you to see us after January 1.

Respectfully yours,
Agnes G. Caffrey

The wheels of the couple's adoption process began to turn, but not without a hitch. In Reverend Shean's multiple roles as provost, and liaison with Catholic Charities and the Charleston Archdiocese, he traveled between the Oratory in Rock Hill, Charleston, and Savannah, Georgia. I can imagine how anxiously Agnes and Al were anticipating a reply from Father Shean. They might have worried that Agnes's handwritten missive hadn't arrived in Rock Hill and wondered whether she had used enough postage. At last, the couple received the reply on Oratory letterhead with the Latin motto *Omnia Omnibus*—all things to all men—the envelope fixed with a long strip of purple three-cent stamps for "Special Delivery."

December 15, 1951

The Oratory
Rock Hill
South Carolina

Mrs. Aloysius Caffrey
202 East Liberty Street
Sumter, South Carolina

Dear Mrs. Caffrey:

I have your letter of December 8th and I must apologize that it has not been possible for me to get down to Sumter to see you earlier than this particular time, and I sincerely hope that you will be patient with the delay in the handling of your application.

I should be very happy to see you on the 16th, but I think it might be better if we were to arrange it in such a way that I see you in Sumter, for the simple reason that I must go to Savannah on the 16th and it would be a simple matter for me to stop in Sumter to see you on the way down rather than have you come all the way up to Rock Hill. At the moment, I shall plan to arrive in Sumter, either on Saturday evening or Sunday morning. In either case, I shall call you upon arrival and I think we will be able to take care of this matter before the week is finished.

With every best wish I am,
Sincerely yours in Christ and St. Philip,
Very Reverend Maurice V. Shean, C.O. Provost

The next hand-penned letter from Reverend Shean is a bit of a mystery. The letterhead is "The Barringer Hotels" for Hotel Richmond in Augusta, Georgia. That doesn't puzzle me because I read the priest traveled between Georgia and Charleston Diocese. But the date on his letter is August 17, 1951—well before adoption communications had begun. The small envelope is crowded. There are two postmarks, Dec. 27, Sumter, SC which overlaps Dec. 18, 1951, Augusta, GA. Father had addressed the letter to "Mr. and Mrs. Aloysius Caffrey c/o Reverend Nicholas Bayard St. Anne's Church 216 East Liberty Street, Sumter, S.C." But the address was crossed out, and a forwarding address written across the left side of the envelope in pencil reads "c/o Tokar 444 W. 58th St. New York, 19 N.Y."—the address of Agnes's parents. Only one purple three-cent stamp is affixed, and there is no New York City postmark. Did the initial recipient, perhaps a secretary at St. Anne's Church cross out "to the care of Father Bayard," check the parishioners' file box for Caffrey, and find an alternate New York address? And after writing in the address, did she realize that the Caffrey's address was across the street and deliver it to Agnes by hand? The mystery letter reads:

Aug. 17-51 [sic]
Dear Mr. and Mrs. Caffrey

If you are angry you have a right to be. I'm very sorry that I did not see you on Sunday. On Saturday in a conversation with Miss Margaret Bayly of Catholic Charities of Charleston, Miss Bayly asked that you go to Charleston for the interview. You would have to come to her or call to make an appointment that would be suitable for you and her. I'm sure that she would not be able to see you on a Sunday.

Miss Margaret Bayley, Catholic Charities of Charleston 86 America St., Charleston, S.C. I have sent the papers to her.

Sincerely,
Fr. Maurice Shean

The next two notes from Catholic Charities must have followed one or two I did not find from Al and Agnes, in their anxious efforts to schedule an interview, and complete the adoption application with all the parties: the Oratory and hospital-infant home, and the adoption agency—Catholic Charities. I cannot guess why no reference was made to making phone calls to expedite the application process.

January 16, 1952

Catholic Charities of Charleston
86 America St.
Charleston, S.C.

Dear Lieut. and Mrs. Caffrey,

Thank you so much for your letter of January ninth. We will be delighted to see you both someday before noon either next week or the week after. We do ask that you come on one of the weekdays, because these interviews have not proved satisfactory on the weekend. We suggest that you arrange permission for a day most convenient for you, but also arrange an alternate day. We will do our best to arrange our schedule here to suit the day you choose. If we cannot, we will do so for the alternate day suggested. We will expect to hear something from you about this shortly. And we'll look forward to meeting you both with pleasure.

Sincerely yours,
(Miss) Margaret Bayley, Executive Secretary

January 18, 1952

Lieut. and Mrs. Aloysius Caffrey
202 East Liberty Street
Sumter, South Carolina

Dear Lt. and Mrs. Caffrey,

Your letter suggesting an appointment for 10 a.m. on Thursday, January 24th will be quite satisfactory for us.
We will look forward to your coming.

Sincerely yours,
Margaret Bayley
Executive Secretary
Catholic Charities of Charleston

The Announcement

Catholic Charities of Charleston
86 America Street
Charleston, 14, South Carolina
February 19, 1952

Dear Lt. and Mrs. Caffrey:

Here is good news! Baby Ruth Ann will be waiting for you in the Infant Home as soon as you tell us you can conveniently make the trip to Rock Hill. She was born on September 21, 1951, and so is nearly five months old. She has brown eyes and dark hair and weighs about fourteen pounds. The baby's nationality background is predominantly Irish and English. Her parents were of average height and medium build. There is no history of advanced education, due more to circumstance than lack of ability. There is no one particular occupation or talent that needs mentioning. As soon as you feel that you can make the trip to Rock Hill, let us know so that we will be able to notify Sister Mathia of your coming. She will release the baby to you on any week day between the hours of 10:00 and 10:30 or 2:00 and 2:30. The afternoon is the only convenient time on Sunday.

When you go to Rock Hill, you will go directly to St. Philip's Hospital, which is on Confederate Avenue. Sister Mathia will go with you across the street to the Infant Home. You will want to take to Rock Hill whatever clothing you want the baby to travel in.

We suggest also that you bring a couple of sterilized bottles for feedings and a well-scalded thermos bottle in which Sister can put some of the baby's formula.

One of our requirements during probation is that you send us a report letter each month. This is most important. If we have not anticipated all the questions you might have, just let us know when you tell us that you are going to make the trip.

With all good wishes, I am
Sincerely yours,
(Miss) Margaret Bayley
Executive Secretary

(At the bottom of the letterhead stationary, *"A Red Feather Service of the Charleston Community"*)

How many times must Al and Agnes have read and re-read this letter, studying the instructions?

The couple was surely over the moon! They would quickly tighten up their plan to make the trip to Rock Hill now that the news of Ruth Ann's availability was in hand.

When Al moved out of the Shaw AFB barracks, and Agnes took the train south, he had their furniture—originally from his parents' apartment—trucked down. Agnes's mother shipped a crib from New York to Sumter. The baby would have to sleep in the front room since there was barely room to make the bed in the couple's bedroom.

Out of the Blue, a Poem in Prose

What did Virgo's stars portend? A prophecy of place and time, a *raison d'être*. On the designated date, September 21, the cusp of Libra the Just, she was pushed into the autumnal equinox. Formed in a fog like a nebula. Delivered in sorrow on fall's first day. Early autumn brought blue asters, sweaters, schooldays, and storms.

The mother and child—placed together by unvirtuous accident—were separated in a single, swift scoop of happenstance. All concerned should be protected. *Our* union of chance was brought asunder by circumstance. Another postwar charity case gave me life and then left in tears. Left me in tears. In a swirl of ambiguity and abstraction, we were severed and left to wonder. The facts of her birth were muddled, muddied by secrets and lies, her name erased, the records sealed. Out of the wild blue yonder, blue like a September sky, like a sapphire birthstone, she belonged to an Air Force couple.

February 27, 1952

It's much like every morning. Maybe the infant's wide, brown eyes follow a swaying oak branch outside the upstairs nursery window as she listens for voices to attend to her. She might have whimpered in empathy to another infant's cry, soothing herself with her left thumb. Then a kind smile, and someone speaks her name: Ruth Ann. The gentle soul who takes her onto her lap brings comfort, and like a hungry sparrow, the baby opens her mouth for the cereal spoon. Her eyes stay vigilant while she nurses from a warm bottle propped against a rolled cotton blanket in her crib.

It seems Agnes and Al didn't ask for details of Ruth Ann's story—my story—the details were undisclosed to them. They didn't question what they were told—that my birthplace was Rock Hill, South Carolina, probably in St. Philip's Mercy Hospital and Infant Home. Since I don't have a clear record of where I spent my first five months, I am given to speculation. My heart aches for Baby Ruth Ann, no matter the caregivers' good intentions; my early months were in institutional care.

Rock Hill, The Oratory and St. Philip's Mercy

The Oratory is a mission run by a society of priests and brothers, a federation founded in Italy by St. Philip Neri (1515–1595). In 1934, the Oratory established a community in Rock Hill, its first in this country, in response to the needs of the poor, many of whom were millworkers. The Oratory invited the Sisters of the Third Order of St. Francis, founded in Peoria, Illinois—who care for the poor and the sick—to Rock Hill to purchase and operate the Fennell Infirmary.

Founded in 1910 by Dr. William Wallace Fennell, a country doctor and orthopedic surgeon (1869–1926), the Infirmary was known to take in foundlings for adoption.

When the Infirmary closed in 1935, the Oratory acquired it with the Sisters of St. Francis and renamed it St. Philip's Mercy Hospital and Infant Home. The Oratory and a home across the street from the hospital, the Infant and Foundling Annex, worked with Catholic Charities of Charleston and the law firm of Spencer & Spencer to place infants in qualified homes.

More information and a timeline of the history of Rock Hill Oratory can be found at https://rockhilloratory.org/about-the-oratory/history/.

This is one of the articles sent to me by the archivist of York County Library, Rock Hill. (Note the spelling with double l's which I've seen used alternately with Philip's.)

St. Phillip's Hospital Adds Children's Annex
March 8, 1951, The Herald, Rock Hill

Work has already begun on a children's hospital annex which will be part of St. Phillip's Hospital in Rock Hill. The annex, which will provide additional facilities for at least twenty-four children, will be in a building directly across the street from the main hospital building on Confederate Avenue. The building which will be used for the new annex was formerly used as a foundling home. Present plans will call for the building to be remodeled so that the entire first floor will be converted into a children's hospital. The second floor will be used by the foundling home. The children's hospital will help fill in an urgent need for additional bed space at Saint Phillip's. *The annex will be a complete unit in itself with offices, utility rooms, portable x-ray, and other necessary equipment for the care of children. A sprinkler system will also be installed. In addition to the work being done at the children's annex, a sprinkler system will also be installed in the main hospital building. This is another step in the remodeling program which has been going forward at the hospital for some time.*

Cost

Sister Mathia, Superintendent of the hospital, estimates that the total cost of the new annex and sprinkler systems will be about $22,000.

Recently, she mailed letters to persons who contributed to a 1948 drive for funds for a new hospital asking if they objected if their contributions were used to help pay for a children's annex. She said today that so far the response has been overwhelmingly favorable to the plan. The 1948 drive actually collected about $10,000, and that money was put in a savings account to be used as a building fund.

Asked if plans for the proposed new hospital had been abandoned, Sister Mathia replied, "No, we haven't given up our plans or hopes for a new hospital. But we realize that it is impossible for us to build at this time because construction prices are high and materials are getting scarce. But we do have hope to get a new hospital in the future."

She added, "Right now we desperately need more space. The establishment of a children's annex will be a great help. That is why we asked those who contrib-

uted if they mind us using the money to provide these badly needed facilities. They have been most kind and cooperative in the replies, and we deeply appreciate their attitude."

The present plant is normally a 65-bed hospital but often takes care of more patients than that at one time. Sister Mathia said the new edition will permit the hospital to take care of at least 100 patients.

~

Homecoming

Early on the morning of February 27, Al warms up his Chevy sedan on the driveway of their Sumter apartment building. He's wearing civilian clothes—perhaps gabardine slacks, a gray raincoat, and a herringbone newsboy cap. His brown wavy hair is clipped close for military service.

Agnes wears a tweed car coat and rubber ankle boots. Her blue, gold, and white cotton headscarf, printed with Army Air Corps symbols, a souvenir of her husband's wartime service, is tied under her chin. She hoists a blue vinyl flight bag onto the back seat. According to the instructions in the letter confirming their appointment, two warm blankets—one is Air Force blue wool—are stacked in the metal-framed car bed, one of several baby items Agnes's mother sent from New York.

They turn onto Main Street toward Columbia via Highway 201. The sloshing sound of the windshield wipers against the wet snow adds to Agnes's jitters. Their appointment with Sister Mathia, Superintendent of St. Philip's Mercy Hospital and Infant Home, is in two hours. In good weather, the trip takes about two hours. They head north to Rock Hill near the North Carolina border.

Since the day they applied in the Charleston office of Catholic Charities to adopt a child, they've been busy with preparations. They've longed for a baby for years, and now the time has come. Agnes is afraid to hope too much, perhaps afraid of disappointment.

I picture Sister Mathia in her black habit and black lace-up shoes as she exits the hospital's front door, approaching Agnes and Al on the wet sidewalk. She extends her hand with a smile. "Pleased to meet you, Lieutenant and Mrs. Caffrey. I hope your trip wasn't too difficult. Should we go across the street? Someone is waiting to meet you."

Sister holds the edge of her white headpiece against the wind, gathers her long, black wool cloak, and steps off the curb. The couple follows Sister on the cement path between clipped shrubs, up the steps into the Children's Annex. Al carries the flight bag over his shoulder.

Once inside the Children's Annex, they climb the stairs to the second-floor nursery, which is a fresh, light green. Soft light filters through the windows. The perimeter is lined with cribs with more cribs in the center, forming aisles, well-populated with babies born and relinquished in St. Philip's Hospital, St. Francis Hospital in Greenville, and in upstate South Carolina maternity homes.

Sister introduces Sister Francella, the baby nurse, a jovial, middle-aged nun dressed in a white nurses' habit. "And here is Ruth Ann!" The baby lies on her stomach with her head raised for her visitors. Sister Francella lowers the crib rail and reaches in for the baby, who is dressed in a pink cotton gown. She faces the baby toward the smiling couple, whose eyes are moist with emotion. Ruth Ann weighs a well-nourished fifteen pounds. Wisps of fine brown hair grace her forehead, and her eyes are dark brown, inquisitive, and serious. She quietly studies the couple and doesn't seem fearful.

Agnes accepts the baby's generous weight from Sister Francella. She says, "As you told me to, I brought a scalded thermos and two sterilized bottles." Al removes the thermos from the flight bag.

"Oh, good!" Sister says, and takes the thermos to the adjacent kitchen to fill with formula. She has prepared a feeding schedule, neatly written in pencil on St. Philip's notepaper.

Using her visiting nurse's training in baby and new mother care, Agnes lays Ruth Ann in the crib for a diaper change. She eases the baby's plump arms and legs into the Carter's terrycloth footed sleeper she brought with a bunting for the trip to Sumter, and snaps it down the front and across the bottom. She tucks the baby into the bunting, then wraps her in the fine blanket that Al's sister, Rosemary, who has been promised the role of Godmother, crocheted for her. Agnes's heart flutters as she picks her up.

Maybe in a warm tone, Sister Mathia says, "Well, Ruth Ann, this is goodbye. We'll think of you often." Sister Francella's eyes well up as she says, "Be a good girl, Ruth! Eat your food up for your Momma!"

Sister Mathia directs to Agnes and Al, "We'll be in touch during probation. We look forward to pictures and progress reports!"

Agnes must have felt butterflies at hearing the word *probation*. From her time in nursing school, she knows that being a "probie" is a time of testing for the big league. Motherhood will be the final exam.

Al shoulders the vinyl bag, and they move toward the door. Agnes takes the steps cautiously with her precious bundle, and Al opens the door to the warming air. Agnes settles Ruth Ann in the car bed and loosens the bunting, arranging the blankets loosely. She stays in the back seat with the baby, and Al cautiously begins the drive south to Sumter. The day has brightened.

February 27, 1952
Dear Rosemary,

We are both not over the shock of being parents. We now have Mary Ellen with us. We took her home Tuesday in a terrible snowstorm. You see, we had to go to Rock Hill, SC, to get her, and this is in the mountains near Charlotte, NC. Mary Ellen is the most beautiful baby in all the world. We feel we have been blessed to be given such a beautiful child. She is not only beautiful but good natured. She smiles all the time. She has big, beautiful brown eyes about the size of quarters. She has his coloring, same color hair, and just as much. Everyone tells us that the baby looks a lot like Al. Al has no buttons on his uniform, because they all pop off when he tells people about his beautiful daughter. I had a lot of company come to see my precious bundle today. We gave her a tub bath tonight in the big tub, and she takes to water like a fish. She loves her bath, but it takes two to give it to her.

February 28, 1952

Here I am again the next day, and it's the same routine again. I thought Al would finish the letter last

*night, but his eyes were tired. He brings home a lot
of paperwork, and this takes up all his evening. He
is in full charge of personnel, because the major who
was in charge is on some temporary assignment. Al
is really working hard.*

*I plan to take the baby out to the base today to
see if I can sign her up as a WAF in the Women's Air
Force. Al is anxious to show her to everyone at the
base. If I'm going to do all I plan to do today, I must
hurry. Don't forget to come down to see your new
niece. I hope Mom and Dad will come soon. They
better or else. I need a babysitter and a diaper washer.
Do you want the job?*

> *Write soon.*
> *Love,*
> *Al, Ag, & Mary Ellen*

A New Life

My family life started in the Liberty Street one-bedroom
studio apartment. From my crib in the living room, I
accepted Agnes and Al's focus and responded to their
playful sounds and songs, their care and attention. Their
soft voices elicited wide smiles and coos. They took turns
holding me and posing for photos. When I fussed, they
picked me up and comforted me.

They might have wondered how many hours I had spent
in my crib before, surrounded by many cribs and many babies
vying for attention. I eagerly sucked my left thumb for self-
comfort. St. Philip's had provided kindness, care, and a scheduled routine, but with a nursery full of infants, the sisters
couldn't give an abundance of personal attention. The tastes

of Pablum, jarred fruits and meats, and vitamin drops were familiar to me from the infant home. I didn't need to cry long before my needs were met: a diaper change, a bottle, or a song.

When I was a child, Agnes she told me that she had feared I might be taken away from her by Catholic Charities, for not being a capable mother. Catholic Charities might well have made impromptu home visits during the probation period, but I don't have access to any notes that may exist in their archives. Surely, Agnes was competent. After all, she was a skilled nurse.

In the spring, Agnes's mother, Julia, took the train down from New York City, bringing more joy, love, and toys: a squeaky elephant, a rubber dog, a cloth clown with a ruffled collar, and a yellow plastic phone rattle. I bounced in a springy baby seat on the living room linoleum or a sunny grass patch in the yard of the apartment building.

This fun lady was called "Nana," and would become a bright star in my life's constellation. She wheeled me in the Carolina spring air in a large, gray baby carriage. It had a hood that could be flipped back or forth to adjust the sun. A neighbor named Mable Bradshaw became friendly during Nana's visit. She flipped the lid, or hood, to better see me, and exclaimed my preciousness in a southern twang, "Isn't she par-ay-shus?"

During my childhood, my grandmother would repeat the story, and tell me how Mable invited us into her elegant home, and took us to a church sale. Nana bought a white porcelain chicken, with gold, glass eyes, that can be lifted from its nest to store candy or other goodies. This story, accompanied by pictures, sparked flashes of memory. Nana always displayed the chicken in her china cabinet, and it still lives in my home—in her china cabinet.

On Armed Forces Day, May 17, 1952, Al was in his tan summer uniform and blue Air Force cap. He introduced me to Major and Mrs. Custer, Al's commanding officer, who had written a fine reference letter to Catholic Charities. I sat up nicely in the wood-handled stroller sent from Nana. Maj. Custer took pictures of our new happy family.

It was all so exciting—the crowd, the floats, the boom of the marching band playing "Stars and Stripes Forever." Everything was big in my wide, brown eyes. The fullness of sounds, the loudspeaker's music that surrounded me, moved me. Maybe it was the new song, "For Me and My Gal!" At a parade a few years later, a swell of sound and music will stir my heart. I'll never forget it: "Love Is a Many Splendored Thing."

Progress Reports

Agnes and Al tracked my progress diligently. Entries in Agnes's white, rayon-padded baby book include monthly photos encircling a featured photo of me, and all noteworthy dates. The first main note is the car trip on February 27, the day I was brought home.

The progress reports that could only be called love letters were sent with photos of me to Charleston Catholic Charities. Now, as I read these letters, typed on onionskin, the choice of words might seem to objectify me, make me still the "other"—on trial—which, in a way, I was. They might seem like the baby had to perform to an acceptable standard. Surely, this wasn't Al's intention but was the mainstream in child development. Nonetheless, Catholic Charities agreed that the baby was in good hands.

April 23, 1952
Mrs. Margaret Bayley
Catholic Charities of Charleston
86 America Street
Charleston, South Carolina
Dear Miss Bayley:

Another month has passed, and time again for a report on the progress of our darling Mary Ellen. She has really progressed quite remarkably, and we still think she is an exceptionable [sic] baby. Since our last report, much to Daddy's delight, the baby has learned to say "da-da," and she has also enlarged her vocabulary to include "ba-ba." We think she is amazing in other ways also. Mary Ellen has learned to sit alone, and lately, she has started trying to stand up in her "Tether Babe." Of course, the greatest news is the addition of two lower teeth to her perpetual smile.

The last day or so, Mary Ellen has not been eating too well, and we were a bit worried. Yesterday, her mother took her to the pediatrician for a checkup and advice about her lack of appetite. The doctor examined her and gave us the simple shocking answer. Our baby was cutting four upper teeth. The doctor also weighed her, and she now weighs 17 pounds, 5 and a half ounces. This was a loss of 4 ounces from the previous week when she had her second series of injections. The pediatrician assured us that this was normal and not a cause for concern.

Mary Ellen takes a daily sunbath, and she now has a beautiful tan color. Everyone who sees her remarks about her wonderful complexion. She loves the sunshine and fresh air and heartily enjoys her frequent strolls in her baby carriage. The baby's grand-mother was down from New York to see our precious child, and she was thoroughly delighted with her. The baby quickly took to her grandmother, and it was a sad experience for Grandmother when she had to leave for home. We believe there is no one in New York City who has not seen pictures of Mary Ellen by this time. Everyone falls in love with her, she is so precious.

We have only a few snapshots of her taken since our last letter; they are enclosed. We took some beautiful color snapshots of the baby, but Grandmother had to take them back to New York.

There is much more to say about our baby. We could write books on her, but this about covers the highlights of her life during the past month.

Sincerely yours,
Lt. Al Caffrey

27 May 1952
To Miss Margaret Bayley,

Time for another letter about Mary Ellen. The months roll by very swiftly, and Mary Ellen is now eight months old. It is very hard to believe. As usual, our report will be filled with praise for the best little girl we have ever known. Honestly, we have been so happy with her that it is rather hard to understand how we ever got by without her. She has certainly completed our life.

Last week, Mary Ellen completed her inoculations and was vaccinated for smallpox. The doctor looked *her over entirely and said she is in perfect health and excellent condition. She weighed eighteen and a half pounds during her examination.*

One of the upper teeth we mentioned during our last letter pushed through the gums, and it is a fine big one. She has several more teeth ready to come out in a very short while. Her gums are sore, but she is really a darling. She is not too fussy when her teeth are bothering her.

She has learned a new trick since we last wrote. Mary Ellen has learned to crawl, and she can go like a speed demon. She loves to get into the bookcase and take the magazines apart, talking like a broken record all the while. She can also stand in her little canvas chair, and she is beginning to use her feet to push herself around.

We have taken her to two parades: Armed Forces Day at Shaw and the iris festival here in Sumter. She is not the least bit interested in any part of the parades outside of the bands. When they go by, she tries to outrival them with a noise of her own. She seriously has wonderful lungs.

She is really a very excellent baby. She cries very seldom and is always ready with a smile. She has her little tricks though, and we practically stand on our heads trying to correct her. One, she is a very picky eater, and we just have to insist that she eat. Second, Mary Ellen loves to suck her thumb. We have tried to correct her of the habit and have it partially cured. The doctor tells us we should not try to stop her, that she may become frustrated. We hope that as time goes by and by our correcting her, she will overcome the habit.

We are enclosing a few snapshots of the baby to keep you posted on her development so you can see

how she is progressing. If we get the opportunity, we
will try to come to Charleston someday and bring
Mary Ellen to see you.

Sincerely,
Al and Agnes Caffrey

Meeting the Family

In Agnes's baby book, she notes the "July 1952 vacation" to
New York. I was ten months old when Al drove us to the
Big City in the new Buick Special. I slept with Agnes on the
Castro Convertible at her mother and father's apartment at
444 West Fifty-Eighth Street. Al might have stayed at his
sister, Rosemary, and her husband's uptown apartment at
10 Cooper Street, the same building his brother, Pat, and
his family lived. Al likely had military and personal business
during the month we were in New York, and I feel sure he
would have visited his former colleagues, the Paulist priests.

The series of photos taken upon our arrival against the
brick backdrop of Roosevelt Hospital across the street from
Agnes's former home express the elation of having a baby.
At last! They were parents and grandparents.

In one photo, I sit at Rosemary's kitchen table, shirtless
and laughing on Agnes's lap. I'm cooling off, playing with
plastic blocks in a white enamel pan of water. On the same
afternoon, Al, in a short-sleeved tattersall shirt, has hoisted
me onto his left shoulder like St. Christopher with the Christ
Child. We're in front of the wide open kitchen window that
overlooks the courtyard and clotheslines. We're both beaming—there must be nothing to fear.

They brought me to their hometown to show me off
to their immediate family and share their happiness, not

to seek approval. Al must have sorely missed his deceased parents then. He would have loved to show them his pride and joy. It does surprise me, though, that the prospective adoptive parents were cleared to drive to New York for a full month with me before I was legally their child. The Air Force couple's approval was all but a given—they had provided the necessary references showing that they were devout, practicing Catholics, as well as Al's church affiliations, having been a Paulist seminarian.

We moved to a roomier apartment as the probation period was ending. Catholic Charities sent this letter to the new address at 9 Orchard Place, Sumter.

Dear Lieutenant and Mrs. Caffrey:

It hardly seems possible that your six-month's probation period will be up this month, but it is and as soon as you find it convenient to do so, you can send us your check for $100.00 made payable to Spencer and Spencer. We will attach the check to papers which we have for Mr. Spencer, and send them to Rock Hill. Shortly after that you should hear something from them. Mr. Spencer will send you papers to sign and have notarized. The final papers will take longer to come to you, but will not in any way affect the fact that Mary Ellen already belongs to you. After the adoption is complete, we will send you a combination birth and baptismal certificate, which will list you as parents.

We have thoroughly enjoyed your report letters and have with interest followed all the progress made by Mary Ellen. We have particularly enjoyed the pictures which you have been thoughtful enough to send. It has been possible to see how fast and how well she has been growing. What is the full legal name by which you want Miss Mary Ellen known?

With all good wishes to all three of you, I am
Sincerely yours,
Margaret Bayley
Executive Secretary

Dear Miss Bayley,

I am enclosing my check for $100.00 made payable to Spencer and Spencer required in your letter of August 13, 1952. It surely does not seem possible that our probation period has ended, but we are very pleased that Mary Ellen will finally be legally ours. We would like you to have Mary Ellen's name shown on her birth certificate and baptismal certificate as Mary Ellen Caffrey. My wife's full name is Mary Agnes G. Caffrey, and my full name is Aloysius A. Caffrey, in case you require these for any legal papers.

Thank you again for all of your kind consideration, and we assure you that we will continue to inform you of Mary Ellen's progress.

Sincerely yours,
Al Caffrey, 1st Lt. USAF

Part Two

A Do-Over

Written and typed instructions from Catholic Charities, character references, the adopters' health history, education, and genealogy sketched on yellow lines. The System is in place for South Carolinian mothers who can't keep their babies. They wait on servicemen in bars, or in the textile mills. Unwed and viewed unstable by the State, many are dirt poor.

"You'll have to give your baby up," the Seamless System says. "A good family wants a child. You can't take care of her." Families, social service agencies, churches, maternity homes, missions, infant homes, doctors, lawyers all make up the System that must work for the good of the state, the good of society.

Vital Statistics has a way to take care of the problem of illegitimate babies. A better way to enumerate these postwar orphans, bastards, and foundlings. A better way to hide the sins of wanton mothers. A way to protect adopters from an imagined onslaught of bereaved birth mothers. "We can protect these worthy parents, and protect these poor babies from dehumanizing labels. Give them a new life! A chance! And in this process, their birth records shall be sealed."

The baby disappears into the ether. "Adoption completes your married life and gives a new life to a lost child." A fine arrangement for all concerned, the System says.

On October 20, 1952, a new version of an infant's life is created. Nine months since she joined the couple—just over a year from her birth—the papers are duly notarized.

The child petitioner is Ruth Ann. In Hebrew, the name Ruth means *friend*. Ruth, a Moabite, great-grandmother of King David. Ann, from the Latin Anna, which, in turn, comes from the Hebrew Hannah, or Channah, *grace* or *favor*.

The child's Guardian ad Litem, Sister Mathias of St. Philip's Hospital and Children's Home, speaks for the child who is known as Ruth Ann, whose rights have been subsumed and sworn over, just as all the babies in her care, the fortunate ones, at least. Neither the child nor the adoptive parents are present. Lawyers, agency representatives, and court officials are present.

The Adoption Decree states:

> *"The party of the first part hereby gives and grants the party of the second part the full and complete custody, management, care and control during its minority, together with the full and complete right and power as one in loco parentis to provide for and consummate the adoption of the said child by such person or persons as in the sole discretion of the party of the second part it may deem proper for the best interests and welfare of the said child."*

By these words and state seal, one life is substituted for another. The adoptive parents are named, and the birth mother is omitted. She was deleted from the process the moment she relinquished Ruth Ann to the nuns in the hospital. By this formal process, Ruth Ann is Mary Ellen. *Ruth Ann* is effaced.

The original, long-form birth certificate is locked away by Vital Statistics; effectively void. In the eyes of the state, it no longer *exists*. The Certificate of Birth and Baptism issued by St. Anne's Church in Rock Hill when the adoption is finalized states that Mary Ellen was christened February 4, 1952, by Father Sharples. Rosemary and Pat, the adoptive father's siblings, are the godparents by proxy. The certificate bears the seal of St. Ann's Church, not the state of South Carolina. The document states that Al and Agnes are the child's parents. It states the date of birth but no hospital, time of delivery, doctor, or birth weight, or the baby's feet impression. Falsified, mythical—was it ever a true legal document?

Ruth Ann loses everything: her mother, her heritage, and her name. Her birthplace is immaterial in this new life with another identity. *Let's say,* she was born in Rock Hill, as it says on the certificate of baptism and birth. Church and state unite in this way. The state keeps the real data. The child becomes fictive, lied about. Rebirthed, rebranded in a court, like a commodity. Exchanged by a new name for a *chosen* child who will fit into a family with the power to perform the Do-over. *Let's say,* were she born of a Baptist, she would *convert* to Catholic. In one fell swoop, Ruth Ann to Mary Ellen. It would have mattered. Names matter. Double names are popular in the 1950s: Mary Lou, Mary Beth, Mary Jo, Sue Beth, Sue Ellen. Ellen Mary is the dead mother of the adoptive father—her new name is an upside-down do-over. A mirrored inversion of someone the child will never know. The infant breathed, bloomed, grew, and was called Ruth Ann for five months. She emerges from the do-over newly certified as Mary Ellen Caffrey. Al's sir-name is a shortened form of McCaffrey, Irish and Scottish—from the Scots-Irish who sailed from Ulster to New York City in the 1800s. Not my clan.

The manila envelope contains a pack of papers, the court records, and the request for payment of the balance due, and good wishes from Catholic Charities. "Best wishes from all of us," and "keep in touch. Send photos!"

Part Three

Working Out Just Fine

This undated letter from Al and Agnes was likely written prior to the court date, October 20, 1952.

Dear Mrs. Bayley,

Since our last letter, Mary Ellen has grown into quite a young lady. She has learned to walk by herself, and now there is no keeping her down. She is the cutest thing walking around the house pointing and looking at new things with oo's and ahh's.

We received the legal papers from Spencer and Spencer two weeks ago. We filled them out, had them notarized, and returned them over a week ago. We are now waiting for final action on them.

It appears things are working out just fine for the Caffrey family. I have received orders reassigning me from Shaw AFB to Athens, Ohio. My new position will be assistant professor of air science and tactics at the University of Ohio. This is a four-year assignment teaching college students in the Air Force Reserve Officer Training Corp. I am scheduled to leave Shaw AFB on 29 October 1952 for six weeks

of training at Maxwell AFB, Alabama, beginning 3
November 1952.

After I complete my training in academic instruc-
tor's courses, I will be sent to the University of Ohio.
Agnes and Mary Ellen are going to New York to Agnes's
mother's home until I finish my training at Maxwell
AFB, then they are coming on to Ohio. Agnes and the
baby will be leaving Sumter on 24 October 1952 if
everything goes as planned. Our new address is Athens,
Ohio. The street number will be 74 South Shannon
Street. We will be there in Athens after New Year's.
In the meantime, Agnes and the baby will be at her
mother's home at 444 W. 58th Street, New York 19,
New York.

Sincerely,
Lt. Caffrey

Nana takes the train to Sumter, and my mother and I travel
back with her to New York City on October 24, 1952. We
stay with her through Christmas. I'm thirteen months old.

Dad reports back to Shaw Air Force Base after comple-
tion of his assignment at Maxwell AFB, makes final transfer
arrangements, signs out of Shaw AFB, and drives to New
York for Christmas. We visit Dad's brother, Ed, and his wife
and two boys in Jackson Heights. Nana and Granddaddy
join us to visit their son and daughter-in-law, Vincent and
Virginia, and their two-year-old daughter in Astoria. Aunt
Rosemary and Uncle Tommy invite us for Christmas dinner
with Aunt Myra, Uncle Pat, and their three children, who
live in the same building. Great Aunt Kate joins us from
the nursing home. Mom's note mentions I received a doll

carriage, a doll in a red dress, a tricycle, and a tiny table and chairs. The gifts are loaded into the Buick's spacious trunk with our Samsonite luggage. My purple tricycle stays behind with Nana for some future neighborhood. I sit up front between Mommy and Daddy, unless I'm willing to lie in the car bed in the back. We leave for Athens on December 28.

Ohio and New York

I have no recollection of this trip into the wintry Midwest but have a few memories of our early days of 1953 in the upstairs apartment of the South Shannon Avenue two-family home. I have a faint memory of ivy-on-white kitchen curtains. Some furniture is delivered from South Carolina—originally from New York—I see it in the black-and-white pictures. Mom, once again away from her mother, with a toddler and a mostly absentee father, must try to adjust.

Photos nurture my memory of our first hot days in Athens. On our tree-lined street, I stand in my kiddie pool in a one-piece nylon bathing suit and pour pool water from my painted tin watering can. I strut in my mommy's high heels and her straw hat, carrying her pocketbook over my arm and wearing nothing but training pants. *Bye bye!*

On July 7, Dad drives Mom and me to Parkersburg, West Virginia, the closest airport to Athens. It's my first plane trip. For weeks, she has been ready to go home to New York for her mother's help and emotional support as well as Rosemary's. Nana and Aunt Rosemary are delighted to have us.

I have glimpses of memory from those summer days. At Nana's apartment, Mom and I sleep on the gray Castro Convertible as we did before. Sometimes I nap on the iron bed in the front alcove. Nana's golden cocker spaniel, Rusty, lies under the high bed with me, and we crunch on Milk Bones. Nana doesn't mind.

Nana lives within walking distance of Columbus Circle. At Central Park I play on the swings, in the sand pit, and feed peanuts to pigeons and squirrels. I hold on to the iron railing that surrounds the zoo cages of African animals. This day, Mom, Nana and I are with Nana's niece, Norma, and my little cousins from Guttenberg, New Jersey.

The asphalt rooftop at 444 West Fifty-Eighth Street had long been a venue for photo-taking when Mom was in her teens. In those days, Nana would peer down into her box camera and take snaps; of her daughter wearing a long, white home-sewn prom dress, Agnes with her best friend, Kathryn, and her cousin Elsie from DC. There are photos of Al in uniform during the War, Al and Agnes when they are engaged, and Mom in her navy-blue visiting nurse's uniform.

In August 1953, Nana and I climb the one flight of stairs to the roof where she hangs clothes on lines between steel poles. The sun makes the black roof tar inhospitable. Nana lifts me onto a new, painted wooden rocking horse and moves me back and forth, stretching the thick red elastic tension band. I'm wearing a short-sleeved, buttoned shirt and long pants, and a cowgirl hat. Nana sticks a plastic pistol into my side pocket, and I look cautious and serious. The caption reads "Mean ol' hombre." After a weak effort to rock for Nana's camera, I'm bawling. Am I frightened to be high up on the roof? Wary of the pungent tar odor? The strange horse? Might I sense we are close to the edge on the roof, as the photo shows? Nana focuses her camera and clicks another photo of me on Dobbin.

We return to Ohio by my second birthday. In the Shannon Avenue apartment, Mom takes photos of me in my party dress, my wavy hair grown to my shoulders. I stand on a kitchen chair and lean on my palms to blow out two candles on an iced layer cake decorated with a striped, cardboard big top tent. An array of clay circus animals marches through the icing. The landlord and landlady, an older couple named Mr. and Mrs. Leigh, are smiling with me.

The Leighs live downstairs. Maybe I was noisy and acted out. Maybe Mom cried and was lonely. What happened? I never heard the details, but Mom said, over the years, that her time in Athens was unhappy. She was treated "mean" by the landlord and landlady, she told me. Did she imagine this bad treatment? "I hated Ohio! Military families weren't liked. I wouldn't stay! I couldn't wait to go home!"

I can say with assurance Mom was obsessed with the quantity of food I would eat. She complained that I said, "I don't wanna!" For as long as I can remember, she thought my behavior wasn't right on a number of issues. Perhaps she doubted the wisdom of my adoption and second-guessed the decision. *Who is this uncooperative child?* Mom seems to have set herself up for my resistance.

As I write this, I feel sorry for her. The pressure she must have felt in her role as an Air Force wife and new adoptive mother with little community, and no help with me, away from her hometown and her mother, and my dad wrapped up in his work, seems to have led her to a near breakdown. Although the adoption had been finalized for months, she feared that I'd be removed from the home. "I was afraid they would take you away," I recall her saying to me through the years. I don't recall hugs from her. Maybe she was afraid to get attached in case I wouldn't be staying.

Dad moved us to an apartment on Mill Street. He must have been concerned that his teaching assignment and absences were contributing to the tension, and wanted to make things better.

IQ

From the blog *Gifted Guru* by Lisa Van Gemert:

> *The reasons not to give IQ tests to young children are compelling... The testing is rarely done for the good of the child... Testing should not be done on a whim, for pure curiosity, or to prove a point... Testing should only ever be done to serve the child, and that is rarely necessary at very young ages... IQ tests... tell you what that person looked like on that day, with that test, with that test administrator, under those specific conditions... I'd far rather have parents relax a little and enjoy their children without worrying... [that] the child will not achieve his or her potential. My first question would be, potential for what? For happiness? For kindness? For love? These are the important things of life.*

In late fall, 1953, I hold my daddy's hand, and we walk down a hall at the university where he teaches. He has told me what we are doing here is important. The first things I see in the room are books on shelves. There are toys and jigsaw puzzles. A man with gray hair and glasses smiles and says my name. He invites me to bring a puzzle to the table at the center of the room, and he sits down there.

Daddy leaves the room, and I climb onto a chair and kneel at the table. I study a colorful, chunky, wood puzzle with pieces shaped like animals and dump the pieces from the wooden frame. I work, fitting the pieces back into the frame, one by one. While I work, the man asks me questions: "Do you like to work with puzzles? What else do you like to play with? Do you know what adopted is?" I answer each question without looking at him because I'm busy. "Yes." "Dolls." "Yes." I tell him a story about the animal puzzle I'm working on. He listens and asks more questions.

Dad reminds me in my early years about the Intelligence Quotient test and how proud they were that I "went to the university when I was two." In the 1950s, the IQ test was a popular assessment of a child's ability. He crows that my results were "above average." I thought it was a strange way of talking. I never understood why it was so important to him or what it would mean about his expectations of me growing up.

Not only was my potential a point of pride for Dad, but it seems to me that he sought affirmation that, despite my uncertain origins, I could achieve, could make him proud. I wouldn't have to be an unknown factor if I could perform to a high standard. It brought my parents relief that I was a normal child. Sadly for me, though, he continued to hold that test up to me and blame me for anything less than the expectations it set.

The doctor might have counseled, "She's very bright and should do well, but, of course, there is no harm in continuing to monitor her behavior and health, considering she was relinquished and very little is known about her. Separation isn't a good idea in these early bonding days, but I understand how the military is a priority. Regardless, it would be best not to leave at this time for both your wife's and the child's sake."

Dad first sought professional help in November for Mom's depressed, nervous state, and for my perceived behavioral issues. Her fears—she'd begun to voice them while still in South Carolina—were around her ability to mother me. She must have had trouble bonding with me—I was still a stranger. Dad made another appeal to continue Reserve Officer Training Corp (ROTC) teacher training by mail in Ohio, as at first he had done in South Carolina—the second time rejected—rather than going back to Maxwell Air Force Base. Here he writes a personal note to his commanding officer, Colonel Graham. On the reverse is the handwritten note from the specialist, Dr. Russell as to why Dad should not got back to Maxwell for additional training:

Dec. 21, 1953
Dear Sir,

At present, my adopted daughter (27 months of age) is undergoing treatment at the Ohio University Branch of the Bureau of Juvenile Research for a feeding and emotional problem. The child's condition has caused my wife such great anxiety that at present she is in a highly nervous state. I have discussed this period of Temporary Duty (TDY) with Dr. Russell, a staff psychologist at the clinic, and he, after consultation with the pediatrician and the psychiatrist involved in the case, has strongly advised against my being away from home at this particular time. A statement from Dr. Russell is attached.

In the past fourteen months, I have been on TDY away from my wife and daughter for approximately sixteen weeks, attending the Academic Instructors' Course and Air Force Reserve Officer Training Corp (AFROTC) summer camp. I feel that another period of separation at this time may prove detrimental to my child's development.

*I have already completed about seven lessons in
the Squadron Officers Correspondence Course and
could reasonably be expected to finish the course by
correspondence.*

A.C.

~

Dear Col. Graham [sic]

*Mary Ellen Caffrey, the daughter of Lt. Aloysius
Caffrey has been under treatment at the clinic since
November 5th. The little girl's problem centers around
a feeding and elimination difficulty involving emotional factors. The condition has been described by
our consulting pediatrician (Dr. Baldwin) as so severe
as to seriously affect the child's health. At the present time, the child is under the care of myself, Dr.
Baldwin, and Dr. Postle (consulting psychiatrist).
The mother is being seen by a qualified social worker.
    It is the opinion of the professional team that Lt.
Caffrey's separation from his family at this particular
time would be ill-advised and would adversely affect
the health of both his daughter and his wife. Lt. Caffrey is regarded as an essential figure in the treatment
of the little girl.*

Harold E. Russell, Ph.D.
*The State Bureau of Juvenile Research
Ohio University Branch*

The Bureau of Juvenile Research was established in 1914
under the auspices of the Ohio Board of Administration.

Children committed to the Board of Administration could be assigned to the Bureau of Juvenile Research for the purpose of mental, physical, and other types of examinations. Bureau recommendations were passed on to the board, which then assigned children to state institutions, foster care, or other institutions.

What might my adoptee status indicate to the doctors about my behavioral or mental health? At twenty-seven months, am I being assessed for a potential delinquency problem? I wonder how close Mom's moods and behaviors had come to creating a self-fulfilling prophecy. Her fears, suspicions, neediness, and anxiety might have put her on the edge of incompetence as a mother.

By the looks of this bureau's mission statement, I might have been evaluated for return to foster care, or institutionalization. Did my mother need respite? Was I on the verge of being given back? Re-homed? It could have potentially come to that. I was being evaluated for the effects of my adoptive parents' care, my suitability, and my inability to merge with the couple.

In January 1954, while Mom and I stayed at the new apartment on Mill Street, Dad flew to Maxwell AFB for six more weeks of training. When he returned from Alabama, he drove us to New York for Easter, April 18th.

After Mass at St. Paul the Apostle Church, Nana and Mom took photos in Central Park of a smiling, well-dressed Agnes, me in a spring coat and hat, and Nana in an elegant print silk dress. I'm wary of the pigeons, as Nana, crouching with her arm around me, feeds them popcorn.

Later in the day, Dad picked up Aunt Rosemary, and we all went to New Jersey, my first trip across the George Washington Bridge. In a town called Teaneck, we met a man named Meisinger, who took us on tour through a "model home."

Dad followed the man's car to a neighboring town, New Milford, parked at the curb, and we all walked up to a red brick house with a picture window. The brick steps didn't have a railing. The unpainted wood front door had windows that climbed like steps. The house was empty and smelled of wood and fresh cement. We looked around the bare first floor bedrooms. In the sunny kitchen, the adults asked the man questions. I later learned he was an architect and builder. Half the upstairs was an unfinished attic.

Outside, Nana and I stood on the freshly paved driveway, and she surveyed the front and side yards that wanted gardens. Young shrubs lined the front foundation, and three young pin oaks—one by the driveway and two at the center of the front yard—were in fresh, green leaf. White birches and two more oaks lived in the backyard. All around us were houses with trees and grass, except for an empty property next door, and this new house didn't have much grass in its sandy soil. On the way back to the city, the grownups chatted about our new home. Something good was coming for us—I felt the excitement.

That May, in Central Park's Sheep Meadow, I'm in dungarees and a corduroy jacket and a tam hat at a stylish angle. But I'm frowning as I lean against the boulder. On the same day, looking reluctant on a see-saw—how was I processing these changes?

Nursery School

Ohio University, Department of Applied Science
July 1, 1954

From the Director of Putnam Nursery School, Julia
N. Rufus.
   ...School opens at 9:00 and closes at 11:30, or
12:30 if she stays for lunch.
   Mary Ellen will need the following articles, and
they should be plainly marked with her name.
   1. smock
   2. small sheet
   3. change of clothing (to leave at school)
   4. rubbers or boots (to leave at school)

In the fall of 1954, Mom holds my hand to and from nursery school, a block from our new apartment on Mill Street. Mom visits and takes pictures of us sitting on our mats at storytime, of the teacher and cook, children in smocks painting at wooden easels, and one of me feeding a dolly in a wooden highchair. She saves a treasure; a paperweight— my handprint molded in heavy gray clay. Her notes in my baby book include the teacher's words, "a superior child..."

~

The Ohio winter blurred into a New York spring, 1955, as my father wrapped up his ROTC teaching assignment. He secured the home back east with assistance from the G. I. Bill, instead of staying on four years at Ohio University.

~

Part Four

Nana and Aunt Rosemary

While I was in nursery school in Athens, construction on our new home was completed. We would share our New Jersey home with my grandparents; a permanent home in a life that was proving to be disruptive for this adopted child, and for my mother, who pined to be with *her* mother. While Mom and Dad are busy with moving preparations, I spend my days with Nana and Aunt Rosemary in the Big City.

Today's adventure is a subway trip with Nana on the D train from Columbus Circle to Greenwich Village, where her long-time friend, Mrs. Toomey, lives on McDougal Street. I hold Nana's cotton-gloved hand as we step through the white-tiled portal into the subterranean world. The underground is a mix of people, peanuts, shoe polish, and newspapers. The air has a peculiar smell. Nana doesn't let go of my hand while she exchanges real money for train money, called tokens, with a man in a booth. She lifts me up, drops one brass coin into a slot, and pushes us through the wooden arms of the turnstile, making a ratchet sound, then a tall gate with bars, and we are near the tracks. I peer from the safety of Nana's side at the blinking light in the dark tube.

People walk this way and that while we wait for our train. I spy a glass jug with a bubbling, swirling orange drink. "I'm thirsty, Nana!" She gives the vendor a coin, and he presses down on the lever to fill a cup with bright orange liquid. He smiles and passes it down to me. Nana says, "Drink it up—the train is coming!" I taste my first smooth, cool orangeade, tinged with the flavor of wax.

Hand in hand, we hurry as the engineer calls out the next stop. When we're safely inside, the sliding doors hiss, then snap shut, and Nana guides me toward a woven rattan seat near an open-window. As we pick up speed, the window breeze builds. On the white wall tile out in the station, black writing blurs. Wall fans whir, no one stands at the center pole, and no one holds on to the swinging grip handles in the almost empty car. My legs dangle from my yellow summer dress as we sway to the click-clack rhythm of track. The ceiling lights flash as we roar through tunnels. Steel brakes screech, and we stop at Houston Street Station, emerging into harsh and jagged daylight and the stifling heat. Nana still has my hand, and we walk to McDougal Street.

She leads me up the concrete steps of her friend's apartment building. In the stale hallway by a wall of mailboxes, we climb the narrow stairs past plaster walls, through the smell of cooking. Mrs. T., having spied us on the sidewalk from her front window, opens to us with a warm smile, and an accent I've heard from old Aunt Kate. They drink tea in the floral parlor and talk while I kneel on the carpet at the coffee table with a glass of cold milk and cookies.

On the train back to Columbus Circle, I bravely sit in a corner seat adjacent to Nana, who doesn't take her eyes off me. There's a gum dispenser when we get out, and I ask, "Please, Nana?" She pushes a penny into the slot, and says, "Hold your hand under it." She turns the crank, and one white Chiclet square drops into my palm, and is instantly in my mouth. I know what to do with the peppermint sugar square.

Like Nana and Granddaddy, Rosemary Caffrey Galvin, my Godmother, is an intrinsic part of my life. I gathered, much later from Mom that Rosemary had been a Dominican nun—an elementary school teacher—and left the convent to marry Tommy Galvin. Rosemary waited until after her mother, Mrs. Caffrey, passed away, in much the same way that Al left the seminary to marry Agnes. Uncle Tommy died behind the wheel on his job as a salesman. We lived in Ohio then, and I never got to know him well.

My aunt is tall and slender with gentle eyes. I love her smiles and hugs, and how she lets me go in the elevator with her and push the button, and go up and down the stairs between her apartment and Aunt Myra's. She hangs her clothes with colorful plastic clothespins. She uses a pulley out the kitchen window to let the clothes dry high above the courtyard on a long double line. She doesn't have to lean out—good, because I worry about her falling. She's a good friend.

I can still smell the newspapers and soda fountain egg creams in the luncheonette on Dyckman Street. Aunt Rosemary selects ice cream from the freezer with the sliding glass top—coffee Dixie Cups for us, and a vanilla cup for Kelly, the old black cocker spaniel we call K. K. He carries his cardboard cup all the way to the building and up the stairs to the apartment. My aunt and I scoop ours with flat wooden spoons. When K. K. is finished with his cup on the kitchen floor, he flips it over. My aunt and I giggle at his antics.

One hot day, we take the subway to Times Square. Aunt Rosemary points up to the Planters Peanut man and the enormous Lucy pop-up Kleenex sign. The monstrous marquees trouble me. We duck into Schrafft's restaurant, and there is Uncle Pat in a big, white apron! He greets us with his sweet, mischievous smile and serves us little sandwiches, and ice cream in parfait glasses. After Aunt Rosemary finishes her coffee, Uncle Pat picks hard candies from the apothecary jar near the cash register and pretends he is sneaking them for me. We say goodbye, and my aunt carries me over to the restaurant where she works and shows me off to her coworkers, the waitresses she calls "The Girls," at Toffenetti's.

~

Part Five

Our Permanent Home

The next time I went to New Milford, New Jersey, our new home on Asbury Street had furniture. I recognized Nana's wringer washing machine from her kitchen at Fifty-Eighth Street, her brown-and-green enamel-topped table, and her stacked, painted-white, wood-and-metal kitchen cabinets, all in the basement of our new home. There were her enamel pots, aluminum pans, old utensils, the tumblers with yellow, black, and turquoise dots that started out as Sealtest sour cream jars, and a variety of glass containers. Mom called them all "antiques," and Nana wouldn't part with them.

Nana splurged on a mahogany bedroom set: a double bed with pineapple finials, a chest-on-chest to hold Grand-daddy's clothes, and a large mahogany bureau with a large, attached mirror. Her yellow synthetic leather armchair with its brass grommets and her gray Castro convertible were in the living room with the coffee and end tables that were shipped from our Ohio apartment. A fancy dining room suite, manufactured in North Carolina, would come the following year, and Nana's dark-red carpet from Fifty-Eighth Street would be replaced by forest-green wall-to-wall.

"This is our permanent home," Dad proudly proclaimed to me, and I got the sense that we were there to stay.

Reckoning

Bergen County is sprouting shopping centers, and new highways attract New Yorkers like my family. Near the intersection of River Road and New Bridge Road is a new Catholic school. A church will soon be built, but now Mass is held in the school hall with folding chairs. I stand with my mother, father, and Nana in the crush of attendees, intent on the glossy cover image of my fresh, white prayer book, and study the colored image of children who clamber into the lap of a kind man sitting on a boulder under a shade tree. His white dress is long, his brown, smooth hair falls to his shoulders, and he has a beard. I can read a bit, but I fidget and whisper to Nana, who tries not to pay attention to me as if in a warning that I should be quiet. Daddy glares in my direction.

By the time we're in the car, I forget what I did wrong, but at home, Dad tells me there is a spanking coming for my misbehavior. His threat hangs in the air and waits while he goes upstairs to change from his Sunday suit. My dread builds, and I moan to Nana that I'm afraid. "I won't let him spank me!" I'm not sure what it means, but I think it will hurt. I hope she saves me, but when he calls, "Come here!" I have to, and he sits on the edge of my bed, pulls me over his knee, and pushes my organdy dress aside. The shame and fear of his sharp slaps sting my thigh, and I yell, spelling out "S-T-O-P!" It's my first bitter taste, a realization of injustice. It's a reckoning with rituals of right and wrong and with the power that my adoptive parents wield. It's a moment when it all changes. I have a mind of my own, and he can't make me do what he wants unless he hits me. I feel angry. This isn't right. *He's not mine.*

~

I remember the time that Mom was vacuuming the forest-green wall-to-wall, and I followed her around like I liked to do, my face close to the comforting hum of warm air that vented from the upright. Maybe I argued about not standing near the open basement door. The sudden crack on my tailbone with her brush attachment made me wail in pain—I hadn't felt pain like that before. My hurt subsided, but not the shock, and I saw her standing near the picture window. She said both matter-of-factly and a bit sheepishly, "I could have paralyzed you by hitting your coccyx bone." Her slight smile might have said "sorry." She didn't say it, though, nor did she hug me. Her volatility confused me, and she never admitted fault.

I'm sure she was a good person, with many fine qualities. She was a talented seamstress, she dressed fashionably, and dressed and groomed me impeccably, but she deferred to her mother in the kitchen. She was empathetic, loved animals—particularly dogs for their unconditional affection. She'd owned one dog or another most of her life. I was attached to her, and especially at ease when she was in good humor. I enjoyed her wit and full, raucous laugh. She could be fun loving, and seemed to enjoy my company at times. But, I learned that she was unpredictable and strong. Her build was more like her father's, a bit stocky, not fine-framed like her mother. Granddaddy was a somewhat simple man, often smiling, and I never saw him angry or lash out as she did.

As an adoptee of newborn relinquishment, I have a need to identify and assemble my life's missing pieces—perhaps filling a need for my misplaced and lost persons—and have collected a composite of cherished memories. Although we aren't genetically related, my grandparents, Mike and Julia Tokar, added immeasurably to the fabric of my life—the warp and weft of who I am.

A Dream Up In Smoke

I'm four, and float and twirl across the green, dotted linoleum floor in a sleeveless plaid dress, happy to be with my grinning Granddaddy, Mike Tokar. He claps for me, and Nana cooks lunch, nods, and smiles. I sing his favorite song:

"Buzzy the Bee went out one day
He put on his coat and buzzed on the way
He wuzzed and he buzzed from daisy to rose
Putting all the honey in his busy little nose!"

One evening after supper, Granddaddy drives me to the soda fountain in his forest-green Ford pickup with a winch in its bed. "We're going on a date!" he says. Strong and gentle, he hoists me onto the red plastic seat of a chrome luncheonette stool and carefully revolves me to the counter. He chats and smiles with the man who makes me my drink. "He's a soda jerk," Granddaddy whispers to me, and he proudly shows me off. "This here's my granddaughter!" He lifts the white china cup from its saucer and sips his coffee with cream, his right pinky held away from the handle, a delicate gesture for a mechanic. I sip my first black-and-white ice cream soda through a paper straw and twist the stool side to side blissfully.

Nana allows Granddaddy to smoke his pipe only at the kitchen table in his corner near the open screen door. His spiky, auburn crew cut accents full, soft, ruddy cheeks. His eyes slit when he smiles. He puffs comfortably, holding the pipe between his lips. I'm drawn to the forbidden fragrance and his leisurely ritual. He taps his pipe on an iron ashtray with boy and girl figures, removes a bristly, white pipe cleaner from a yellow cardboard pack, threads it into the pipe stem and the bowl, and dislodges the pungent spent tobacco. I don't mind doing this for him but prefer to shape and twist the wiry cleaners. I pinch moist, earthy tobacco from his leather zip pouch and fill his pipe for him. He strikes the red tip of a wooden match on the red-and-blue cardboard box, and puffing, he lights up. "Blow it out," he says. I do and stand back from the sulfur wisp.

Granddaddy and I cannot read or write much. Sometimes we practice our names, but we mostly draw. He keeps his pipe cleaners, other smoking stuff, paper, and pencil on top of a pine cabinet next to his kitchen chair. Nana also lets him keep some heavy gears in a shoebox behind the cabinet's sliding doors. Gears are for machines, I know, but Granddaddy draws circles with a thick pencil, tracing the outside and inside around the rippled edges. With a gear pressed to the yellow-lined page, he connects circles end to end or overlaps them in a way I now know is called *concentric*. He is quiet and serious when he draws, holding his forehead in his left hand. Nana says he is "concentrating," so I draw quietly with him. I believe the circles are important work because he has told me, "I'm working on a car for you." The drawings stay in his cabinet until Nana cleans it out when he's at work. "He'll make new ones," she tells me.

Nana and Granddaddy have a tractor trailer repair shop on Hudson Street, called M&F Automotive, for *Mike and Family*, with my mother's brother, Vince. Sometimes, Nana brings me into the city on the bus. She works in the office loft where she answers the phone and does the "books." I sit at the big metal desk and help her by slipping coins into wrapper rolls. I love how Nana yells out the sliding window down to the shop floor, "Hey Mike!" when there is a phone call for Granddaddy. I love that my nana is a boss lady.

Once, Granddaddy drives me in his pickup truck. In the shop, Granddaddy points to a frame high on the cinder block wall. It's the welded chassis of a car that will someday be mine. He says, "When you're a teenager, you'll drive it." He lifts it and sets it down on the concrete floor to show it to me. I can barely see it as a car.

Years later, I learn he called it Petchie, a nickname that meant to him that it would run without fuel—by perpetual motion. During his pensive moments in our warm kitchen, he works on an unsolvable puzzle of gears. I could not have understood my car was his pipe dream.

Garden Shadow

Nana's slim, five-foot-two frame belies her strength and stamina. She stands before the wide mirror of her mahogany dresser, hastily brushing and swirling her fine, sandy-brown hair into a French twist, and shapes it with hairpins. Her plain, soft style is perfection in my five-year-old eyes. I may have once seen her wear woolen slacks to shovel snow but never shorts or trousers in the garden. She pushes the rotary mower, plants, and prunes in crisply ironed, hand sewn, pastel summer dresses.

The year we move in, Nana reads a notice in the paper about a man who collects peat in a rowboat and sells it on the bank by the old draw bridge called Overpeck in the place we now know as The Meadowlands. She says, "I want to feed the shrubs and put in grass seed. Our soil is too sandy," and she brings me along on the adventure. The man loads as many burlap bags of peat as can fit into her blue Nash Rambler convertible. "You can help by staying out of the way!" she says to me. I smell the sharp bog water as it sloshes against the man's moored boat. Nana pays the man in dollar bills.

Nana lifts the burlap bags, maybe three or four, one at a time out of the car to the backyard, cuts them open, and sprinkles the fresh peat around the yews, hemlocks, azaleas, and mountain laurel shrubs. She scatters the spongy, brown peat moss into her new flower beds and on bare patches where grass hasn't sprouted.

I shadow Nana around our new yard, and we make gardens together. She shows me how to dig out lawn weeds by the root with a paring knife and put them in a brown bag she calls a "poke." I'm not afraid to get my fingers dirty, and I want to be like her.

"Would you take care of them?" she asks me at the nursery as she adds pots of yellow and orange lantana to her order. I assure her I will, and we return to Asbury Street and get busy planting.

Part Six

Sacrifice to Serve

My Air Force dad had already been away from us many times, but I was first aware of what his career meant when he told me that summer, "I'm going to Iceland." I shivered at the sound of such a cold journey. He must have felt he could leave with peace of mind since Mom and Nana were happily engaged in the new home. "I'm going to be an adjutant to the general," he said to me, and closing his lips he smiled into his rosy cheeks as he did when he was proud of me. I liked the sounds of the words *adjutant* and *adopted* and *aide-de-camp*. I glimpsed a time when Mom, Nana, Granddaddy, and I would be in our new home without him. "I'll be back before you know it." I would turn four, and he'd be gone through the winter.

I stopped sucking my thumb at night when I was four. Attempts to "correct" this habit hadn't succeeded until I settled into our new home. I wouldn't say I was a carefree child. When I wasn't at physical play, I was introspective. There were signs of a worrying "nature" early on.

Mom enrolled me in ballet classes that fall on the other side of town, maybe on Main Street. I remember she drove me to a wood frame building with outside stairs up to the studio, and I wore a black leotard and white leather Capezio slippers. She said I wasn't graceful—it might have been a tease to boost improvement—but it made me feel self-conscious.

My ballet recital was in early December, and I wore a pink tutu and sparkly crown. My sandy-brown corkscrew curls came to my shoulders, and talent scouts came to the dressing room after the recital to talk with the girls and moms. I guess you could say I loved the limelight.

We had Christmas without Dad in 1955 because he couldn't come home from Reykjavík.

Nana and Mom made it wonderful, nonetheless, with a decorated tree and Nana's prized ornaments from the 30s. Of course, there were toys, dolls, even a doll bassinette. I bet Mom missed Dad. I can't recall being conscious of his absence until I found out I was chosen to be on the television show *Name That Tune* with Mom in January. I guess I was picked for my familiarity with many pop songs, for my speech clarity, and maybe my ringlets.

Nana took me to Arnold Constable for a pastel organdy dress with a crinoline and a dress coat. Mom sewed her dress for the occasion, a Vogue pattern for a tailored wool tweed sheath with a white collar and big, black buttons. She fashionably tilted a black, velveteen tam hat with a black feather. She wore modest black heels. The two of us posed for Nana in front of the fireplace, then she drove us to the bus stop on River Road. We took the number 21 bus, and Aunt Rosemary met us at the George Washington Bridge Terminal and hailed a cab for us to the TV studio. She pinned corsages on our coats in the cab.

From the stage, I saw Aunt Rosemary in the first row, beaming beyond the klieg lights. "I could have died from stage fright," Mom told me years later. I was excited, with no performance anxiety that I can recall. The master of ceremonies, George DeWitt, instructed me and my competitor, a boy about my age, to run to the bells when we heard the song play—we were too short to ring them—and call out the title. There was "Jingle Bells" and "Winter Wonderland," maybe another, and I must have won because I was told I would be on again in January.

Nana and Granddaddy watched us on the black-and-white console TV in the living room. A cousin captured the show on Super-8 film and mailed it to Dad in Iceland, where he proudly projected the show onto a conference room screen for his associates. He later told us he was sad that he couldn't be with us.

Despite missing "Paper Doll" on the second round, we were asked to be on *Stop the Music* with Bert Parks in March. I won Necchi sewing machines—a child-sized and a grown-up model—saving bonds, and cuff links for my dad.

Family Together

Dad's homecoming before Easter, April 1, 1956, was illuminated by his smile, and the gifts he pulled from his B-4 bag. There were Hummel figurines for Nana and Mom. Dad took out a creamy-white plastic console-style television set, about six inches tall, and when he wound a brass key on the back and turned a little dial on the front, twinkling music played, and a tiny ballerina in a pink tutu twirled to the "Skater's Waltz" behind a TV screen. It was a unique German music box—a souvenir from my recital and television performances that Dad missed and saw only remotely. To me, the TV music box signifies our separation. I still keep it in an old suitcase of memories. Its gilt trim broke off long ago. There would be no more ballet lessons. A single stage portrait remains of me in my pink tutu.

That summer was a child's dream as I explored the empty lot, cycled up and down the sidewalk to the corner at Graphic Boulevard on my purple trike, helped Nana in the garden or with the laundry, or cooled off in the basement playing records. I spent untold hours with my little friend, Janet Kay Nelson: lunching at each other's homes, dressing up in tutus—hers blue, mine pink—posing for Nana's camera in the yard, and flying, pumping, and singing on Janet's swings.

I don't think Janet had been in a ballet recital. She was three to my four when we met in play, and her sister, Joyce, was just a baby. Janet and I squeezed through Nana's young arborvitae hedge, back and forth between the yards. Mr. Nelson had assembled the impressive swing set from iron pipes; long, sturdy chains; and wooden seats. It was held in the ground with poured concrete. The swings made great carnival rides, and we used leaves for tickets. Maybe I had seen a carnival ride queue on a TV cartoon.

Mr. Nelson was a carpenter, and his workshop was his garage. He built and installed a cupboard in our upstairs bathroom. He was low-key with a nice smile. He often held a cigarette in his mouth while he worked. He sometimes chuckled, like he enjoyed us children. He didn't mind if we walked in the sawdust. Mrs. Nelson sold Chevrolets in a town near the Hudson River. She was the first mother I knew to dress up and go to work. I loved the Nelsons like a second family.

I started kindergarten at Ascension School the fall of 1956, and turned five. Nana drove me in the morning, and picked me up for lunch. I'd change out of my blue jumper, white blouse, and saddle shoes, watch TV, or help Nana. That was when my life was perfect and uncomplicated. Everything was music, make-believe, and adventure—the self-fulfillment of a child's expression.

At my kindergarten graduation, a stage production followed diplomas. I held hands with Gary C., and we sang "Toyland," a rite of passage. Aunt Rosemary had taken the bus in from New York to stay overnight, and she stood proudly with me for pictures in front of Nana's flowers.

Dad and Mom finished half the basement as a rec room in mid-century style, painting with whimsical primary colors. Dad laid red-and-white checkerboard floor tile. They hung a red mural designed by Constance Depler Coleman, "Bar Hounds," featuring stylishly dressed, animated canine characters—beverages in their paws—being served by a shaggy dog barkeep. Dad crafted an eight-foot redwood bar to complete the look, and stocked it well.

Uncle Pat drove Aunt Myra and their three children and Aunt Rosemary for a little housewarming in our new rec room, to admire my parents' handy work. Life-long apartment dwellers, they enjoyed an afternoon in suburbia. Dad donned a white bartender's apron, tying it in the front to serve snacks and highballs. A photo shows my elder three cousins and me sandwiched on the sofa, the mural behind us, my legs dangling. I have no recollection of another such basement gathering with them, but they were with us almost every Christmas.

Mom, Nana, Granddaddy, and I piled into the Buick, and Dad drove us out to Pennsylvania on a summer weekend. Nana's brother, Pete Ballas and his wife, Jean, were raising a large family at the farm in Pogue where Julia Ballas,

Nana, lived as a girl for a time. She'd been taken in by an old widower uncle, to help on his farm. Everyone was poor in those days, and they did what they had to do with very little means.

I fetched eggs from the rustic hen house and waded in the creek with Mom's nieces and nephews. I fell asleep upstairs by an open window that screened out mosquitos but let in a stillness that amplified the plain call of a whip-poor-will. The night was so clear that the stars danced toward me, where, wrapped in patchwork, I snuggled on the floor next to Nana. Mom and Dad slept in the big iron bed in what, long ago, was the old uncle's bedroom. I don't know where Granddaddy slept.

We visited the dairy farm of Granddaddy's sister, Mabel, and her husband, Elmer, near Middleburg in the Susquehanna Valley. We didn't stay overnight there, but I did milk a cow, and I fished in the farm pond with Granddaddy. On the way home to New Jersey, we drove through the glorious Hershey rose gardens. Nana bought one rosebush and found space for it in the trunk. It was a wonderful family trip.

Part Seven

Away from Home

"We'll be moving to Texas!" I heard the grown-ups talk and felt Mom's anxiety. I shed brave tears when my ringlets were sacrificed to a pixie and Buster Brown bangs. I remember sitting in the barber chair at Mom's longtime hairdressing salon, Nick & Nick, in New York. Mom wrapped the long ponytail of my sandy brown hair in waxed paper and tucked it into her pocketbook for safekeeping.

With long goodbyes to Nana and Granddaddy from the back seat of the Buick, Dad began the drive. The worst parts of the two-day trip to Texas were the high, winding roads Dad called "hairpins" that tractor trailers barreled around. Deep under a Tennessee mountain, we stopped to tour Ruby Falls. I was afraid the elevator would plunge deep into the rocks and feared the narrow ledge we walked on in the caverns. I gripped Mom's hand as we looked in awe at massive, icicle-like growths and in terror at the crystalline, watery depths next to the trail.

Dad's orders for Foster AFB in Victoria, Texas, would prepare him, a newly minted captain, for a ten-month tour of duty in Tokyo. A brick two-bedroom duplex was our temporary off-base quarters. The yard was unimproved—

no flower garden like Nana's—and I proudly built a rock garden with loose stones I found at the bottom of the driveway. Two boys and a boxer named Roger lived in the attached house. Their mother was an Air Force wife, too, and she let us cool off in the three-foot pool outside their back door. In the intense heat, I preferred to stay indoors.

Blue Bicycle

Fall of 1957, before Dad left for Tokyo, he drove me to Sears Roebuck in Victoria and pointed out a blue, twenty-six-inch J. C. Higgins cruiser like the one he'd seen in the catalog. "Here's the one we'll get. Do you like it?"

Wouldn't any six-year-old be impressed with such a beautiful bicycle for her birthday? The purple tricycle I'd pedaled up and down the sidewalk in New Jersey couldn't compare to this grown-up's bike. "Yes! I like it!" I nodded and clapped in glee. "I can ride it, Daddy!"

He hoisted the bicycle into the Buick's ample trunk. A brace of training wheels was attached. I can recall the handful of times the two of us went out for fun without my mother, and this was one. She said, "I stay away from bicycles ever since I fell off when a dog chased me on the dirt road. I was your age."

On the driveway, I stood astride my new bike while Dad adjusted the seat and handlebars. "Okay, go ahead. Start pedaling, slowly."

I felt strong. I pushed my legs down, right, then left, my fingers wrapped around the white handlebar grips, my arms flexed to steer forward on the sidewalk. The pecan tree ahead on the next lawn looked far away. Beyond the neighbor's driveway was unfamiliar terrain.

"Stop here." Dad helped me off and reversed my bike toward our house.

Back on board, the wobbling training wheels frustrated me. "I don't need them! I can't turn! I can only go straight!"

Dad agreed that they could come off when we were back on the driveway. "Okay, push off! Pedal!"

His hand was flat on the rear rack, and I picked up speed and confidence. He guided me into momentum and advanced me through my first imbalance, slow trotting beside me. He was handsome, and he smiled with his full face when he relaxed. I laughed fearlessly into the breeze. I trusted him not to let me go until the right time. He coached, and I heard him behind me in the wake of my cycling stream. "Hold the grips tight. Keep the handlebars straight! Now turn a little to the left—to the right! Steer! Keep pedaling!"

I had it! The moment he let me go was imprinted on me. I was ready to fly.

⁓

Dad came through the door dressed in his blue uniform and cap, carrying his B-4 bag. We hugged and kissed, and he put his cap on my head. He was home for Christmas on leave after his first three months in Tokyo. Mom set up a small tree, and there were a few wrapped packages under it, though not as many as at Christmas with Nana. Dad brought a silk, red-flowered kimono for me and took pictures, my bobbed hair like Buster Brown, crossed-legged on the scooped, white vinyl chair with my Betsy Wetsy doll from last Christmas and the new Revlon Doll Aunt Rosemary brought with her from New York—she flew down to Texas for a few days. The high-fashion doll wore lipstick and had her tawny brown hair pulled back; her nails were polished red. "Revlon" had a coat with a fur-lined hood, turquoise toreador pants with a red cummerbund, and a white silky shirt. She was a big hit!

Aunt Rosemary and Dad left after New Year's, and I was back in first grade.

In the Beginning

In Our Lady of Victory school, Sister Mary Raphael leads my first-grade class in a call and response from The Baltimore Catechism. "Who made you?" "God made me." "Why did God make you?" "God made me to show his goodness and to be happy with Him forever in heaven." Sister says that *reason* is the beginning of mankind's troubles. We must have faith.

Sister tells us that our first parents, Adam and Eve, lived in a garden. I learn that life is hard because of the selfish mistake our first mother made. Eve was tempted by the snake, the devil, the red man with horns and tail, and she ate the apple God told her and Adam not to touch. I assemble the myths and images. I learn that if a baby dies before she is baptized, she goes to limbo, the cold place that has no love and no parents.

I worry I might die when my fever and cough warrant a doctor's house visit in early May 1958. The rash on my chest and the red, spotted throat makes his forehead furrow and say, "Red measles." He tells my mother, "She should stay in bed and rest her eyes. Give her orange juice and the two prescriptions I order for her. No school until she's better."

Mom calls him again, and he says to me, "Now you've got a case of the German measles—very contagious! Your glands are swollen, and you still have a rash and infected throat. You'll have to stay in bed longer, I'm afraid. No school until your throat is clear and your cough is gone." I found out I had back-to-back cases of measles, Red and German.

In bed, I read *Winnie-the-Pooh*, my first hardcover chapter book. I work in exercise books sent home by my teacher, play "Go Fish" and "Old Maid" on my bed with Mom, absorb myself with dolls and their furniture.

As I recover, I get on Mom's nerves. She takes down the flyswatter from the top of the fridge and swiftly makes sharp contact with its metal handle on my backside. "Keep it up and you'll get more!"

Texas was my year of firsts: first grade, first bicycle, first chapter book, first big sickness, and First Communion in May. And I heard about the girl I first was. Dad stood near the head of my bed, and Mom gripped the maple acorn foot post as if it might fly away. I knelt on the bed and dressed Betsy Wetsy in her flannel robe. Dad said, "You know we adopted you, don't you?" I nodded without looking up from Betsy. "We loved you, and chose you. There was an accident, and the others were lost. You had nobody, and we took you home." I noticed, and reacted. *Why didn't I have anybody? Where are they?*

But the story was over quickly, and I was under the covers with my doll. My mind raced. *Adopted* was a word I knew from how my aunts and uncles treated me like a star, the difference to my cousins, the boys and girls of Dad's brothers who all looked like each other. In a way, I knew they were born, but I didn't think of myself that way. *Adopted* meant *different*. Now it might mean *missing*.

I wasn't ready to make sense of this new information. The story ended but wasn't complete. I held a pang of sadness in my heart. Began to question. Pushed back against perfection. Doubted I was the star I was supposed to be. Being different meant losing everything. I was uneasy with the thought I got away unscathed from this accident. A twinge of survivor guilt, perhaps. *Who are the people I belong to? Where are they? Who is this mother? Is there another real me? A girl other than in my father's color portraits? Where did the other girl come from? Who is she?*

In a flash, I'd gone from the innocence of unknowing—not knowing—to knowing more than I could fathom. I now knew less than nothing. When Dad and Mom left the room and said goodnight, I was different from the girl I always had been.

I was alone in my bed. *Alone in the world? What harm have the lost ones come to? The woman and man who do everything for me aren't really mine?* I tried to connect this new story with the part that made me comfortable, with the love and need of the family I called mine.

I better not ask questions. Questions might make them want to bring me back where I came from, or they might be sad at my questions. It didn't seem right to ask about the lost ones. The story was going deep into my chest. It sank inside me to my heart. Since I had no names to talk about them, I couldn't form a picture of the lost ones, not like I did when I thought about my friends, my dolls, or myself. I answered to a name. Names had meaning.

"Ask me no questions, and I'll tell you no lies," I'd heard Dad say, and I asked few.

A scrim of doubt, even shame, began to grow over me. When I thought about the "accident" that happened around the day I was born, I asked to hear the story of my homecoming: the day my parents brought me home from Rock Hill in a car to the tiny Sumter apartment they told me about. The story made Mom smile and made me feel good too. I would veil the new story—bury it—the one about another family that was gone before I had a chance to know them.

I was trying to find my place in the only family I knew—keen to see the differences between me and my mom and dad. I started a habit of ruminating. *Was there something more to know? Something about the accident?* I couldn't bring myself to ask.

Penance

I examine my conscience as I kneel in a pew with my classmates and wait for the green light above the door, the signal it's my turn to go in to see Father. I mull over easy sins to perfect my confessional performance. Five times? Too many. Two? Not enough. Disobeyed my mother three times, lied to my father four times.

I blink as I enter the dim, wood-paneled booth and push the door into its latch. The priest wears aftershave like other men. I can see his profile, his chin in his palm, his eyes closed behind the decorated screen that separates us. I kneel and bless myself. "This is my first confession," I say. I know it's not his.

I hurry through my rehearsed confession and wait for the judgment. I have fibbed to Father. I say the Act of Contrition, and he gives me a penance of a few Hail Mary's. He makes the sign of the cross through the screen. The dusty spot, a smirch of sin in my chest where my soul lives, will be clean.

Come Holy Ghost

On Sunday morning, May 25, 1958, Mom fastens a fine chain with a tiny gold cross pendant around my neck. A prayer book with a blue-cloaked Mary on its glossy cover is in my white leather clutch pocketbook. Shiny, crystal rosary beads are tucked into a white, hand-sewn brocade pouch with a snap closure and a white, embroidery-edged hanky. The details of that day are captured in lovingly beautiful photographs taken by Dad. Dad's portraits of me, and me with Mom, are lovingly beautiful. My Communion dress puffs over a crinoline slip. I wear white nylon anklets; pristine, white patent-leather shoes; and white lace gloves to my wrists. A white nylon mesh veil drapes behind me to my waist; the frill-covered plastic crown is embedded in my short, brown curls. I feel more special than at other times when I'm wearing a new dress. My mother has styled and curled my short hair.

First Communion Mass is celebrated at the Foster AFB chapel for Our Lady of Victory School first graders whose fathers are stationed in Victoria. We've rehearsed and fasted. The choir and congregation sing "Come Holy Ghost." Two lines: bride dolls on the left and boys in clip-on bowties and jackets on the right as we face the altar. We press our hands together, fingers forming steeples pointing heavenward. We begin the procession to the first rows of pews. During Mass, with something like matrimonial nerves, we fidget with our rosaries, veils, and bow ties. Sister Raphael motions, and we file out, row by row, to the Communion railing. My stomach tenses when Father's gold robes rustle as he bends in front of me, holding his gold chalice. I'm surprised that the host is tasteless and firm on my tongue, and I distance it from my teeth as we've been instructed. I mull the disc-like wafer around my cheeks and trace the impression of a cross with the tip of my tongue. I swallow when it softens and digest the dogma.

Summer in New Milford

When first grade ends, we drive north to Nana and Grand-daddy. Spending the summer in our New Jersey permanent home is the better alternative to summer in the Deep South, but I don't hear about the advantages. I only know I love my grandparents and have no idea what will be next for our family. The neighborhood maples, oaks, and cherry trees are in full leaf. Nana's gardens are bursting with blossoming plants. Her pink and red roses climb and tumble through the sturdy white trellis Dad built for her when he returned from Iceland. Nana has lined her garden beds with hybrid roses, annuals, and a few perennial flowers. The lawn is lush, soft, and deep green. The earth is sweet, and birds are everywhere. So different from Texas!

I can see my mother is happy to be with her mother in our *real* home. My parents tackle home improvement projects together, since Dad is on a well-deserved leave. The body of the house and the trim need to be painted and stained. Inside, the window sills have to be shellacked, and the baseboard heater covers have to be painted. There is painting and wallpapering to be completed in the living room, the stairwell, and upstairs. The second upstairs bedroom is finished, and I move in opposite my parents' room. It's spacious like theirs, with ample closets, dormers, and two windows—mine facing west and north; theirs south and west. My parents and grandmother work seamlessly together. Nana had already wallpapered the dining room and her hallway and bedroom by the time the new dining room set came, before we moved to Texas.

I'm busy with Janet and Joyce most of the time, staying out of the way from all the industry. At night, we all watch TV together in the living room.

Lady Liberty

Around August 10, 1958, for my mother's thirty-sixth birthday, and Mom and Dad's thirteenth anniversary, Dad drives us to lower Manhattan and the South Street Seaport, and we board the ferry to Liberty Island. Mom and Dad take pictures of each other with me, the three of us looking happy and relaxed in the harbor breeze. Mom wears a stylish dark print sheath she sewed, and modest heels. I have on a navy blue pleated skirt with a middy sailor shirt and tie.

I'm not at all relaxed in the Statue of Liberty. I resist tearfully when they want me to climb the winding narrow stairs, but Mom insists. Dad lifts me to the observation window, and I glimpse our height above New York Harbor; the green mass of her profile so large, so close. Terror strikes like the night on our New Jersey driveway when Dad lifted me up to see the moon and stars. I only want to flee.

Part Eight

Transfer to Louisiana

It breaks my heart to leave Nana and our home. But Dad has a new assignment in Alexandria, Louisiana, at England Air Force Base. As usual, I have no recollection of moving day—we go directly into another brick ranch off base. The house on Dennis Street isn't a duplex, like the one in Texas, and there's a little more space. The neighborhood is good for bikes, and there are lots of kids to play with. Everything is new again. The church and school are called St. Francis Cabrini. Mom goes to Brownies with me one night a week, which we both enjoy.

Dad and an Air Force associate investigate "UFO sightings." One exploration leads them to an abandoned country house down a dirt road with a shed covered in wild roses. Dad drives me out there one hot day to show me a litter of puppies rolling around in the shed with no momma dog in sight—wiggly, black-and-white critters. "What do you think? Do you want one? Which one?"

I'm charmed by one of the chubby pups, and Dad carries him to the Buick, assuring me that someone will come for the rest of the litter. At home, it's up to my mom to feed, clean, vet, and deworm the puppy, but she falls in love too. I name him Rascals, and this fox terrier is my best friend.

Arlen Needs a Home

Dad pulls the Buick up in front of our house on Dennis Street on the Saturday morning before Easter. He walks around to the passenger side and opens the heavy door. A boy who barely reaches the window clutches a brown paper grocery bag by its thick fold and steps down, grinning. Mom and I come out of the house to greet them. Dad smiles when he says, "This is Arlen. He'll spend Easter with us."

Arlen's smile reveals the space where his two front teeth should be. My permanent teeth have already grown in. Arlen is pint-sized with a gravelly little voice that has a twang. Most of my life has been spent in the Northern states, and like my mom and dad, I don't have a Southern accent. I've been excited since Mom and Dad told me to expect a playmate this weekend. I recognize Arlen right away. He's a first-grader in St. Frances Cabrini School, six years to my seven. He lives in the children's home next to the school.

I'd been curious about the stone mansion and what it is like for the children who lived there—children without parents—until a family took them to live in their home.

The last time I'd heard my father say something about a boy, I was in first grade. He told me about a baby, Michael, who was in the nursery when they picked me up in Rock Hill. Dad said he and Mom passed Michael by because Mom wanted a girl. They brought me home to their apartment instead of Michael. I had forgotten this story until Arlen came to visit.

"Do you want to ride my bicycle, Arlen?"

"Sure!" he says.

My bike is too tall for him to reach the pedals. He needs a smaller bike. We toss sticks and run around with Rascals.

I take Arlen around the backyard, showing him the vine-covered cyclone fence that neighbor boys and girls climb in search of adventure beyond. I pretend he is my brother.

Mom calls us in for sandwiches—baloney on white bread with mustard—and glasses of cold milk. I like that Arlen is at the kitchen table with me, Mom, and Dad. I've thought about the story of an accident that separated me from the family I would have had and brothers and sisters who might have been mine. Maybe he is my real brother. Since hearing Dad's story when I was six, I look in the mirror differently, wondering what my other family looks like. I wish hard that Arlen will stay and be adopted like me.

Dad helps Arlen run a bath, and Mom gives him a new pair of cowboy-print pajamas so he won't need to wear the faded ones he took out of his paper bag. His toothbrush is wrapped in tissue paper. We are both ready for bed, and Dad tells us to say our prayers. Mom has made up the pull-out couch for him because our rented house has just two bedrooms and one bathroom. Still smiling, Arlen scootches between the fresh sheets under the blanket. In my bed, I wonder if Arlen is afraid of the dark. I close my eyes and make a wish that he will stay with us.

After Easter Mass, Arlen and I stay outside in the warm spring air while Dad goes in for his camera. Mom lets Rascals out and brings us our bountiful baskets. We'd ogled them in the living room before church but must wait even longer to sample our candy after breakfast. Mom wants pictures of us with the red brick as a backdrop.

"Say cheese!" Dad takes a picture of me with Mom in our dressy clothes, and Mom takes one of him with me. He takes a few of Arlen and me with our baskets and the cloth bunnies Mom gave each of us. Arlen's bunny is dressed in blue jeans and a straw hat, and mine wears a calico dress and bonnet. The side of Arlen's too-short, yellow, cotton tattersall shirt has come untucked from his tan pants, and no one tells him to tuck it in. His straight, sandy hair blows across his forehead, and his smile is wide and happy. *I love Arlen.*

We can't wait any longer! Arlen and I hurry through our bacon and eggs, and rummage through in our baskets for loose Hershey's Kisses, little pink-and-blue foil-covered eggs and bunnies, and the hardboiled eggs I'd decorated with Mom. A giant, foil-wrapped chocolate bunny is nestled in synthetic green grass in each of our baskets. Mom hides plastic eggs, holding jellybeans, that pop open around the living room, and we search under a lampshade, behind a chair, and under a couch pillow until we find them all.

It feels like a bigger family, and I hope and hope. If my mom and dad say we can, Arlen might stay and be my little brother. Today, I won't disagree or fuss about anything. If I'm very well behaved, Arlen might stay. I don't want this day to be over and start to feel the way I always feel when I worry. In the kitchen, I beg Mom, "Please let him stay with us. Arlen is too sad to leave."

There is no explanation—he can't stay. "He has to go back after dinner," Mom says.

Arlen carries his brown paper bag with his church clothes, his old PJs, and his toothbrush. Dad carries another brown paper bag with Arlen's Easter basket, what's left of his candy, his new pajamas, and the boy rabbit to the car. Arlen waves out the window, and Mom and I wave back. I don't want Arlen to see me cry, so I wait to cry in my room for the brother I can't keep.

What if Mom and Dad don't want to keep me? What if it doesn't work out for us? Would I go back to a children's home? Is Arlen's family dead? I ask myself because I can't ask my parents. I don't want to upset them. Each time I see that cold stone building next to my school, I wonder about Arlen, if I could be returned, or if I will live with Arlen. My habit of overthinking has begun—the whys and why nots of an adopted girl.

Souvenir of Faith

Dad is in Paris for six weeks, and returns with a palm-sized memory from the gift shop in the Notre-Dame Cathedral. The tin-hinged case is shaped like a book, with the cathedral's form in relief on the surface. I trace my fingertip over the metallic spire, towers, buttresses, and round window Dad calls a rose. I pinch the case's latch and let an orange glass rosary ripple through my fingers.

At a sweltering Louisiana school-day morning Mass in St. Frances Cabrini Church the next day, oscillating fans whir breezes down both side aisles. The girls on each side of me press against me like they want to pop me like a blister from their pew and out of their church. They must be jealous of my crystalline rosary beads and the unique case. Mostly, I think they hate me because I'm an outsider, a stranger. I don't know their names. It's my fourth school and sixth state. I hold my space defiantly. A quiet but heated competition is being waged in our pew, while the blue-veiled lady—the Notre-Dame of our church—watches over us from the front of the church. At the rear, the nuns wield their weighty, black rosary beads.

I'll lose my souvenir someday soon. Misplaced like me, it slips away, like the faith that is mine to lose.

On the Move

Second grade is over, and we drive to New Jersey in our Buick Special for the summer, just like after first grade. The square metal Coke cooler is wedged on the floor in the back, full of ice, soda bottles, apples, oranges, and sandwiches wrapped in waxed paper. A pair of plaid, red-capped thermoses—one filled with hot coffee, one with water—stands in a matching metal-handled carrier next to the cooler. Napkins and a bottle opener are stored in the center compartment. I can still smell the inside of the water thermos, and plastic red cup. Mom spread a green and white floral oil cloth tablecloth over a wooden picnic table for a rustic roadside lunch of ham or baloney sandwiches.

We watch for flashing neon "vacancy" lights through the rain, and finally Dad pulls under a motel office canopy. Key in hand, he strides to the room to check for cleanliness, then moves the car to a space in front of the room. Mom carries Rascals, sneaking him in under a jacket. I follow her, and Dad carries in one piece of leather Samsonite luggage. We soon lie back in two double beds to watch a fuzzy, black-and-white TV show, maybe eat another sandwich. We're eager for the long second leg of our road trip to be over.

Borrowed Ladder

At home in New Jersey, one summer evening, my neighbor friends, Janet and Joyce Nelson, and I are working on a large United States puzzle on their Florida room picnic table. We all hear Rascals bark like crazy—he hardly ever barks. Through the jalousie windows, across our adjoining yards, I see Nana hurry along the back of our house and disappear as she turns at the corner of the garage. *What has happened to Rascals? Why are there sirens?* I realize Dad is painting the cedar peak of the new garage extension. Suddenly, Mom is at the door, but she doesn't come in. Sounding scared, she asks Mr. and Mrs. Nelson, "Will you keep Mary Ellen for a while? There's an emergency! Al fell off the ladder!"

I remember the sick, fearful feeling in my stomach. "He might die!" Mrs. Nelson tries to calm me, saying, "He'll be alright, don't worry." It's no use. I'm a morbid worrier. I can't stop talking about my fear that Dad's fall will cause his death, even though I know little about what has happened.

Mom follows the ambulance to Hackensack Hospital, and Nana comes to the Nelson's to retrieve me. On our driveway, I watch in a mix of horror and fascination as Nana gathers up Dad's strewn canvas drop cloths stained with his blood and brown paint. "Dad borrowed the Orel's wooden ladder," she says. It seems odd to me. *Hadn't they used a ladder to paint the second floor white trim about a year ago?* I never knew they borrowed. Our neighbors are grandparents, too, and so sweet. They wouldn't have realized their ladder had a weak rung and would break under Dad, causing him to crash to the driveway head first.

When Mom returns from Hackensack, she says, "He was taken to Fort Dix Army Hospital." Or maybe, she says, "He went to the Veteran's hospital in New Jersey." He's gone for weeks—maybe six. Summer just keeps on going without him. When he comes home in a military car, he seems different to me. He has a deep red scar on the side of his forehead. He wears a sling, since his shoulder was broken. I am glad he's home—I wasn't sure I would see him again.

Julie Ann

In the summer of 1960, we're north with Nana and Grand-daddy when Mom gets a long call on the yellow wall phone one afternoon. When she hangs up, she exclaims to Nana and me, "That was Catholic Charities! There's a baby girl ready for us!" We make wide Os with our mouths at this great surprise. I didn't know we wanted a baby, but Mom is wide-eyed, so the news must be happy! "We'll have to leave soon!" Dad and Mom prepare, and within a few days, we're on our way back to Louisiana.

Before they can pick the baby up at the maternity home in Shreveport, there's much to do in Alexandria. Mom and Dad shop for a crib, linens, a baby dresser from Montgomery Ward, bottles, a sterilizer, bundles of cloth diapers, crib toys, baby gowns, frilly dresses, bonnets, and ruffled diaper covers. So much fun to get a baby!

On the road to Northern Louisiana, I'm not thinking how this day is like the day they got me from Rock Hill, although they might have mentioned it. I'm dreaming along the road from the countryside to the city, thinking about what it will be like to have a baby in our house. I'm terrified when the Buick rumbles loudly on the tracks of the narrow railroad trestle bridge over the Red River.

Dad parks, and we climb the big steps into a waiting room with long curtains and old-fashioned cushioned furniture where a smiling nun greets us and directs us to have a seat. "I have someone waiting for you," she says. I look around at the Blessed Mother statue and crucifix on the wall. There is a smell of heavy, old fabric. I busy myself swinging my legs on an easy chair and whispering to Mom.

Sister comes through the door holding a tiny baby in a

blanket, and I stand close to see the baby better. I feel my heart get happier when Sister holds the infant girl toward us. She passes the baby to Mom, and Sister and my parents are talking to each other. I want to hold her, too, to take in as much as I can of the sweet little one, curious about this baby who is going to be ours. We are told she was born on May 22.

"What will her name be?"

"Julie Ann, after my mother, whose birthday is May 19."

"How wonderful!" Sister says. "And now, you're a big sister." She turns to me. "You'll be a helper to your mother, won't you?"

I nod and smile. They tell me to sit so I can hold Julie Ann on my lap. She has bright, blue eyes and a sweet face. I love her already. Mom takes her back, and the adults go to the desk to write while I wait.

We all say goodbye to Sister, and now our family is larger by one. There is a soft vinyl car bed for Julie on the back seat, and Mom sits next to her. I sit up front, a proud big sister, next to Dad on the trip back to Alexandria.

I help my mother with Julie as much as she lets me, holding her on my lap and I love her sparkly blue eyes. In our parents' bedroom, a musical angel and mobile of stars hang over the crib, and a porcelain infant Jesus night light glows on Julie's dresser. I love to watch her get bathed in the kitchen sink, her silly, toothless laugh, and how she kicks and splashes. I feel useful folding her cloth diapers.

Mom holds Julie's hands to stand and take her first steps and notices she doesn't put her soles down, walks only on her toes. The pediatrician fits Julie with sturdy white shoes that have a bar between them. Mom says, "She has to keep her legs and feet straight at night." This makes me feel sorry for my baby sister, but she is good natured and adjusts to the brace. I later learn from Mom that the baby's high palate and bone structure are from her teenage mother's vitamin deficiencies.

Not to Be Mentioned

I must have seen at least one expectant mother by the time I was eight but make no clear connection to a baby, and I don't recall the word "pregnancy" being mentioned at home. Mom uses "P.G." for short, in a strange, embarrassed way. Looking back, maybe she distanced herself from the condition she'd never experienced. I was rarely around her big family of cousins and don't remember seeing their infants. I hadn't put together questions about my three-month-old sister's origin. It was all so mysterious.

I didn't ask for details about my first story, the one where they picked me up from the infant home in South Carolina. There was nothing much to say about my beginnings, I guessed.

I couldn't comprehend that I was born from a woman. I assumed that babies came on the scene by some kind of intentional or forced removal from their chubby mothers. My parents gave me "The Visible Woman" plastic model for Christmas, but Mom didn't look at it with me. I was expected to figure it out for myself, like the amateur chemistry set I got that year. It was up to me to grasp the hows, how-tos, and whys. A curled-up, plastic baby was included in the female anatomy kit, but apart from thinking it sweet, I didn't pay much attention to its placement in or exit from its clear, cold mother.

What did I understand about a nine-month gestation? I learned at six that I had a mother who was taken away in some accident, but I wasn't conscious of a connection to her. Neither did I have a physical bond with my adoptive parents. Nana let me snuggle with her on her bed to watch TV when we visited her. Mom was not a hugger. Dad planted a kiss on my lips when he returned from long trips, but when he was home, he only said, "Good night. God bless you and take care of you," with no kiss. Mom never kissed me goodnight.

One evening, I sauntered into the living room with a blown-up balloon under my shirt. I was being comical. Bad move. Dad lunged from his chair, outraged. "Don't ever do that again!" He swatted his newspaper at me like a bad puppy. I let my playful pregnancy drop from its place against my body, and I burst into tears. I ran to my room and hid, embarrassed and confused. What had I done wrong?

I know now that Dad saw that it was his duty to protect both of his adopted daughters. He probably believed—likely knew—we were born of "wayward" mothers. He would have to control me, or else I could turn out like my birth mother. Might not my parents have decided, since they had to rely on other women's foibles to form their family, to simply love these girls enough to overlook that they were not theirs genetically and embrace them with all the love they might have given a child of their own? Couldn't they have relaxed and assumed that their adoptive girls would turn out fine if they only listened to their needs and loved them?

Prancing in front of him with my make-believe replete womb had triggered my dad. He couldn't ignore or chuckle it off because that would give my disgraceful behavior tacit approval. He had to shame me, make a statement about illegitimacy.

In the history of the adoption industry, the term "disturbed" was used for unwed mothers. In my adoptive father's puritanical, patriarchal view—how he was raised—they were undeserving of their babies, especially when compared to a devout Catholic couple. The rescue institution of adoption came about to protect us all from the shame of our origins.

Devotion

At bedtime most nights, we pray the family rosary. Dad, Mom, and I kneel in front of the blue-and-green plaid daybed at England AFB. I shift to put less weight on my left knee, bandaged after a spill with my bicycle. Dad says to "offer it up" for the souls in purgatory. A three-foot-tall plaster sculpture of infant Jesus hovering on the end table wears silk, satin, and velvet, one of several sets of garments Mom has sewn for him. She says, "The third joyful mystery…"

At eight, I make a miracle. I am witness to the supernatural as I play on the floor beside my bed with my cigar box of religious paraphernalia. My pink plastic phosphorescent crucifix has recharged under the dust ruffle. It glows green and flies away from me a few feet! I call saying, "Mom! It flew by itself!" She believes it too.

Spirit Down to Bone

The chaplain visits our house on Schilling Drive to bless us and our newly adopted baby. He gives me, the big sister, a cellophane packet with a holy card stapled to it of a haloed, dark-skinned man who wears a white gown and brown robe.

"This is Blessed Martin De Porres," Father says. "He lived hundreds of years ago in Peru and cared for the poor. Ask him to pray for you."

I thank him and agree, reading the tiny typed label. *Linen touched to the bone of Blessed Martin.* I feel sure I'm not supposed to touch the relic. I imagine Martin's bones, his white skeletal leg, and his martyrdom. It would be a sacrilege.

Before too many days go by, I open the packet and take out the teeny waxed square. I touch it, examine it carefully, and put it back in the cellophane envelope and into my cigar box of religious articles.

When I was four, I visited Great Aunt Kate, Dad's and Aunt Rosemary's father's sister, in the New York convent nursing home. She answered our knock, walking with a blackthorn shillelagh, her long, black dress like a habit, her back prominently hunched. Her sparse, silver-blond hair was pinned back in a bun, and her kind eyes were clouded by glaucoma. There was just one chair in her thimble-sized room, but no one sat in it. She sat on her bed, and so did I. Aunt Kate said to me through her tight smile in Irish English, "Let me see what I have for you." With wrinkled fingers, she felt in her nightstand drawer to find a few holy cards, a Miraculous Medal of Mary, and black rosary beads. She was the last of the eldest. Her tokens of faith were bequeathed to her nephew's shadow child. I kept them in my cigar box.

Part Nine

Endings and Beginnings

I began fourth grade at Our Lady of Prompt Succor in Alexandria, and it seemed that soon Mom was boxing up the dishes. Dad built a pine platform, a car bed to fit on the seat behind the driver, where Julie could sleep. If my parents mentioned this next step, I was oblivious. I don't recall talking about the big trip or the change ahead of us. I had noted their vagueness over things *I* wanted to talk about. Perhaps it was a commonly used parental tactic to control the child's expectations, to keep her living within the moment.

I had come to anticipate impermanence in our family. Hypervigilance—what I now believe is an adoptee's self-preservation instinct—shielded me, kept me quiet, or egged me on and antagonized me. I was either a girl of quick reactions or I hung back, clueless of what would come next.

Christmas in New Jersey

We were going to Nana's house for Christmas. Mom had sewn a cushioned mattress for Julie's new car bed. She dressed her warmly and laid her in it. "Go to sleep," she told the seventeen-month-old. I stretched my legs under the wooden platform and turned onto my left side, my back to my parents. Still wearing my pumpkin-colored parka, I cuddled against the thick seat back and soon was submerged in dreamland. Julie and I slumbered to the boat-like rhythm of the big green Buick. Through towns and mountains and behind the rumbling engine hum were the omnipresent, reassuring, muffled, reverberating voices of Mom and Dad.

Without much prattle from Julie, and since Rascals was well-behaved next to me or up front on Mom's lap, there wasn't much to distract me on the long trip. I never read in the car and don't recall bringing books on trips. I had a plastic puzzle with numbers you slid until you got them in order. I know I sang aloud or in my head. I don't recall my parents playing the radio on trips. I must have been beyond the threshold of bored, relaxed, in a meditative zone, a place of peace and comfort. Anticipation lost.

Patches of snow lay in some roadside woods. Dad said, "We'll soon be at Nana's house! Won't be long now!"

When we exited Route 4 in Bogota, we were in the suburbs, and the crossroads looked familiar. As I pressed my face against the cold window, my breath fogged in the fading light, and I remembered my pink-papered bedroom next to Nana's, her African violets and violet floral wallpaper. I wondered if my baby toys, like the striped metal top, were still behind my sliding closet door.

Christmas lights in primary colors decorated porches and eaves, and Dad pulled into the driveway. There were no Christmas lights up at Nana's; a single white light greeted us. There was a little snow on the lawn, and there would be more to come to build forts and snowmen with the neighbor children. It was Julie's first northern winter and her first visit with Nana and Granddaddy. Their laughter and love warmed us as we went into the family home.

Nana carried in an armload of firewood. The small, white logs she kept in my pinewood doll cradle with its brightly painted peasant figures were all that remained from the native birch trees that grew in the backyard when we moved in. I was fond of those birches and the squiggly green, then brown, worms I used for doll meals, the way rainwater pooled where the lower branches joined, and the yellow leaves in the fall. I had noticed that adults didn't like the messes trees made and wondered that the pin oaks had survived the ax and saw with their annoying acorns that attracted squirrels. The trees gave breeze and shade in the summer to put our lawn chairs under, and a single clothesline was nailed between them for Nana to hang throw rugs or Granddaddy's work pants, supplementing her square umbrella clothes hanger.

Nana shifted the kindling and added a couple oak logs when the fire got going. She poked them to settle into the grate and made the sparks fly, simple tasks she learned in her childhood. I sat beside her near the hearth, and we chatted like we always did. Julie's eyes were everywhere, fascinated by the home and the flash of hearth flame. It was her second Christmas—she was seven months old for her first in Louisiana.

The eight-foot balsam tree had leaned against the outside kitchen wall on the patio since Granddaddy loaded it in his pickup at a local Christmas tree stall. Mom and Nana carried it together up the back steps, paraded it through the kitchen, and positioned it in the red metal stand in front of the picture window. They tested the chunky, multicolored lights. Standing on a step stool, Mom strung them through the fragrant branches. I helped her and Nana decorate, handing green and red glass balls with a wire attached to each as high up as I could reach. Nana gingerly placed her paper-thin Eastern European ornaments from the 1930s. I loved them all and still have most of them: the boy in peasant garb; the brightly colored peahen with stiff, white tail feathers; the girl in a faded blue coat; and the Hindenburg dirigible. Percolating candle lights were favorites, and they fascinated Julie. Nana and I arranged tinsel on every branch to the top-most angel that Mom placed.

Nana and Granddaddy gave Julie Ann her first doll, Cry Baby Cathy, who wore a pink gingham party dress. I remember when Nana gave me Betsy Wetsy for our first Christmas in the new family home.

The torn wrapping paper gathered up and the boxes closed and stacked under the tree, it was time to get dressed for Mass. I put on the pale-blue, shirtwaist dress with a bouncy slip Nana gave me and posed for pictures in front of the fireplace.

Aunt Rosemary rode in from the city with Uncle Pat and Aunt Myra for dinner. Uncle Pat always brought holiday candy: brightly striped hard peppermints, foil-wrapped Santas, and gold-wrapped chocolate coins in red mesh bags from his place of work, Schrafft's. He always snuck a little money into my hand with a mischievous look. As always, Aunt Rosemary brought me a doll, this time a Madame Alexander Little Women Amy. Mom gave me the Jo character. I was sure everyone showered Julie, too, but I was more interested in what I was getting, as grown-up as I was.

My parents took me to the Steinway & Sons showroom on Sixth Avenue in Manhattan. In Louisiana, I had begun piano lessons, and the teacher said I showed promise in voice and keyboard. I demonstrated my novice touch on a Baldwin Acrosonic, playing a tune called "The Spinning

Wheel." Mom and Dad looked so proud of me, sure this was a good purchase for a girl who showed some musical talent. From my early childhood, Mom and Nana fostered my love of melody and rhythm. I'd progressed from stacks of yellow and red 78s, ballet recital and musical TV performances, and school chorus to a rented piano at England AFB, and now this brilliantly toned instrument graced our living room at the side of the stairway.

Miss Gertrude was an officer of the National Guild of Piano Players and an imposing woman with a stern demeanor. She rang the doorbell promptly at six every Thursday evening. "You must use discipline," she said. She demanded one full hour of practice daily. Mom complied, enforcing after-school practice. I played Kohler and preparatory pieces, exercising my fingers for future Mozart, Bach, and Beethoven.

The Crossing Guard

After the holidays, I returned to Ascension School with classmates I remembered from kindergarten. In the second half of fourth grade, I recognized the names and some faces of Frankie, Jack, Sue, Denise, and Peggy, whose parents didn't move from place to place, and they seemed to remember me. I wore a blue serge jumper, white short-sleeved shirt, blue clip bow tie, and beanie as I did in kindergarten. A Dominican sister taught geography, arithmetic, spelling, Spanish, music, art, and composition. It was one of my best school seasons. I thrived in my schoolwork and, with Nana at home, even kept to a homework routine as well as piano practice. I was especially diligent at Spanish vocabulary. Mom was proud to tell me that Sister Mary Paul asked her if I might be Spanish since I was so tan and was taking up the language so well. *Sister knows I'm adopted, doesn't she?* I was curious why I was guessed to be ethnically Spanish and why that might be since I was told I was Irish. Once again, I was confused about my origin. Mom's comment didn't go further. I didn't think it was my place to talk about such things. It felt embarrassing at age nine to talk about where I came from.

The moving van has come with furniture, boxes, and... "My bike is here!" My blue bicycle stands on the front lawn for the first time in New Jersey. It's ready to ride on familiar neighborhood streets and sidewalks. When the ice has melted, I take it on the mile ride to school from our Asbury Street home. I'm feeling brave and powerful the first time I take my bike to school and am proud to stand it among the others in the bike rack.

I clutch the handle of my book bag in my left hand and steer with my right. Dad gave me a Cordovan leather briefcase for Christmas. It rocks back and forth.

The soft-spoken, tall, lanky crossing guard at the corner of Hoffman and Berkeley is a retired policeman named Bill. He's concerned about the clumsy way I carry my book bag on my bike. He says, "I think it might hinder your balance and steering. I'd like to make something for it, a hanger to go between the handlebars. I think I might have something to make it in my garage. What do you think?"

"Yes, okay, thanks!" I nod to my new friend. I walk my bike with him across Berkeley and ride off to school.

The next morning, he shows me the crafted metal hook he has made for me. "Here it is. I hope it works." He explains how he bent and shaped the pliant metal into a double hook. He attaches it in the place between the handlebars where my dad had attached the ill-fated safety lamp and buzzer a year or so ago. "Go ahead and try it." Bill hooks my book bag by its double handles and stands back, satisfied. "Well, I think that may work!"

I thank him. We walk my bike across the street as we always do, and I take off for school.

At home, I stand my bike on the kickstand in the garage as usual. I mention my new book bag hanger to Nana and Mom and how the crossing guard made it for me. I don't tell Dad about it- because I don't know what he'll say. He might not notice it. When school closes for the summer, I forget about the hook and explore the town with my new bike-ridng girlfriends.

Rascals, Goodbye

Six months pass while Dad has been going to New York City and Virginia's Langley AFB, his headquarters as an Intelligence officer. He has new orders. We'll leave for Tokyo and live there for three years. I don't want to leave my neighborhood, my new friends, and Nana. My head swirls with the changes that are coming fast how can I keep up? The school year will soon be over, and there's so much going on at home.

My best playmate, Rascals, has canker sores in his ear, Mom tells me. He's been at the vet for days, and I ask at the dinner table, "When is Rascals coming home?"

"He isn't coming back," Mom says.

Stunned, I cry out, "Oh, no, no!"

"He wouldn't be able to make the long plane trip in the cargo hold. His ears hurt him too much. The vet said it would be best to put him to sleep."

I knew of no pets being euthanized and am horrified.

I howl. "He's not coming home? Not coming with us? My friend is gone forever?"

I run from the table, in anguish and confusion, and down to the basement where I know I can find his brush. Devastated and crying in pain, I sit on the floor, pulling out his little black-and-white hairs from his brush to attach to and feel his presence. It's too much for me. I don't get sympathy or condolences from my family. Maybe they are sad and sorry, too, but there's not a word of apology or comfort.

Too many losses at age nine. Houses, play spaces and yards, friends and classmates, people and places I'll never see again, and now Rascals, my sweet terrier friend. The deep wound of a family I've never known. Gone. I'm heartbroken. I have to bear the pain on my own. Adults have all the power—even over life and death.

Part Ten

The Transient Military Life

In a social media forum of "Air Force Brats," I read exchanges that hint at their difficulty coping in a transient military life. Here are a few snippets. The names are changed.

Lisa

I learned early on not to form any close relationships. The first few times I did, my heart was broken, and I decided no more. I stopped letting myself get close to anyone.

Flo

My dad retired when I was in eighth. It was my first off-base school. I remember the summer before meeting people who had known each other since kindergarten. It took a while to grasp.

Susan

My dad retired from the Air Force when I was fourteen. I have few memories of friends. We only stayed two to four years at bases at a time. When I went to a civilian school in the eighth grade, I knew no one.

Everyone else knew everybody and who was kin to who. I never felt like I fit in.

Joe
I'm sure our adoptive parents didn't have a clue and thought they were doing everything right. My dad was strict and used a belt, but my adoptive mother was the same way. She had a buggy whip. It was mostly emotional. There was just no affection. I never felt like I belonged.

The Tokyo Years

On June 15, 1961, Mom, Dad, and I wave to Nana and Granddaddy from the macadam of the Idlewild Airport runway, and they wave back from the observation window at the American Airlines gate.

In San Francisco, a blue vinyl airline diaper bag is slung over Mom's right shoulder. I hold her left hand as we follow Dad, who carries two-year-old Julie. My baby sister's pink cloth summer hat is tied under her chin, and she wears a fancy dress under her lightweight blue coat.

My shoulder-length hair is braided, and powder-blue ribbons match my summer dress. I feel like a grown-up carrying a tan raincoat over my arm, but my light-blue-and-white saddle shoes and white anklets are those of a nine-year-old. Mom's pleated, white skirt and the hem of my dress catch the hot runway breeze as we board a wide, luxurious Pan Am Boeing 707 to Hawaii.

In the visitors' center in Honolulu, we stretch and shop while the jet refuels. My vial of Waikiki sand is as close as I'll get to the beach. More military families board the plane, and we depart wearing orchid leis. I brought a Mutt and Jeff coloring book, a twenty-four box of crayons, and a sketch pad for the long journey to Tokyo International Airport, and I amuse myself as clouds float below us. Jet engines roar and sparkle in the sun glare.

In the limo on the way to the Hotel New Japan, I realize I left my brand-new, blue-banded Cinderella watch tucked in the airplane seat pocket and that I'll never see it again. Loss and change are part of my life, I'm starting to learn. Dad says, "You are old enough to be responsible for your personal property."

I take in my first impressions of Japanese culture: the tatami floors in the guest rooms, a Pachinko game at Dad's American friend's Japanese-style home, a Japanese restaurant in the Ginza where a lazy Susan stands in the center of our round table. We sit on floor cushions and use steaming towel rolls before the meal.

At the hotel, there is a lush garden where I see a chain of submerged iris in a stream with a wooden arched bridge suspended over beads of glistening little ponds. Shades of blue coalesce, and dragonflies dart and hover on water lily pads. Ladies with their black hair piled and fastened wear brightly patterned silk kimonos. *Geta* shoes make a gentle clop of wood on wood.

A driver delivers our Buick to us when the freighter docks. Dad drives us from western Tokyo to a big gated housing complex called Washington Heights in central Tokyo, a community for American military families. There's a grammar school, movie theatre, nondenominational chapel, base exchange (BX), officers' and enlisted and family clubs, and two large concrete swimming pools. We can drive to Tachikawa or Yokota AFBs for groceries, clothes, and housewares at a commissary or big BX, and Tachi as it is called, has a hospital and a dispensary.

Our furniture comes in a van from the port: living room chairs, Mom and Dad's bed, our dressers, clothing, kitchen supplies, my bicycle, toys, and dolls. All the rest of our belongings are with Nana in New Jersey. My parents do their best to make the bare, two-story house comfortable by adding simple dining furniture and a sturdy rattan living room suite from a local craftsman. Twin beds for Julie and me come from "Supply." My parents surprise me with a used upright piano so I can continue my lessons.

More than anything, I want to be outdoors with other children. The wide streets and sidewalks lined with flowering cherry trees, the grassy courts surrounded by shrubbery, give us space to run, play ball games, ride our two-wheelers, and fly on the smooth school parking lot on ball bearing skates.

The grove of black oak and pine that is my sacred, quiet space stretches behind the housing units in our American enclave at the heart of Tokyo. I roam the mossy ground and wide dirt paths, a Druid under a domed canopy. Under dapple of summer or bare winter chiaroscuro, we carve hearts in tree bark and peel cambium scars to renew initials. In the summer rain, we wear sockless boots to wade in the grass downstream.

Japanese cicadas—*higurashi*—appear after the rainy spring, and their chirping music crescendos into the summer. They congregate on the trees and slip their papery brown shells as they grip their claws to the rough bark. We lift them, lifeless but threatening, to wear on our shirts like scary badges.

At the far northern edge of the woods is a ledge with wide gullies where big boys bike daredevil down the swale or fly over with a long rope swing and drop into deep mounds of collected oak leaves.

This forest is a fragment spilling over the fieldstone wall from many acres of trees in the Meiji Jingu Shrine inner gardens. Many acres of evergreens had been planted in 1926 to honor the spirits of the emperor and empress, the last rulers of Tokyo's Edo period. Although I never visit these gardens, the wall undulates along the edge and banks and borders my sanctuary.

That first July and August, I'm often alone, and I explore on foot or bike, riding between roots of mature trees and around boulders. This foreign place, this urban forest, becomes familiar. I feel a connection, a solace, a reverence for this rooted space. In my view, the place is honored, reverently groomed by the Japanese caretakers. I too feel respect for the quiet woodland and the old stone wall.

Sometimes, Dad drives our big Buick "outside the gate" and parks on a narrow side street in the Shinjuku shopping district. People wear both Western and Japanese clothing, and we are carried through the hustle and bustle. Men stand or squat in doorways, smoking. Demure women are alone or in pairs; some carry babies on their backs and hold cloth or straw shopping bags on their arms. I catch the bright red of symbols, the stark strength of black letters on white—advertisements I cannot read.

My stomach growls pleasantly to a blended aroma of street food: steamed yakisoba noodles, fried and grilled dumplings, grilled rice crackers, and skewered chicken yakitori mingle, and we enjoy a light meal on the go. I savor the time our family has with Dad when he is feeling relaxed, when he's not under pressure or traveling.

On the counter in a souvenir shop, a smoke plume

from a spice and floral incense cone spirals and trails, then diffuses among the customers. Perhaps we hear the newly familiar sound of gentle koto strings, a twinkling music box playing "Sakura," the hugely popular song "Sukiyaki" crooned by the young man, Kyu Sakamoto, about a man's memories, or "Ue o Muite Arukō" ([I] Shall Walk Looking Up) and whistling as he passes to keep from crying. Mom chooses a kimono-clad geisha doll in a glass case and a flowered red paper umbrella, *wagasa,* with bamboo ribs, waterproofed with oil. My allowance of a few yen, plus a little extra from Dad's pocket, might buy a few tiny glass animals, a pair of painted wood peg Kokeshi dolls, or a handcrafted Hakata character figure doll in folk dress.

Dad shows affection toward me when he brings me one evening to the Children's Day celebration outside the rear gate. It's a quick trip, just the two of us, and he buys me a crispy fried treat and a pair of jointed plaster baby dolls, one with a pink robe and one with blue. Their noses and mouths are painted, their eyelids open and close, and their pretty eyes are fixed.

In fifth and sixth grades, I ride the military bus with other girls from Washington Heights to the girls' academy, the International School of the Sacred Heart (ISSH). The school Sisters teach French conversation, music, English grammar, arithmetic, art, sewing, religion, and geography. There is no conversational Japanese class, but I pick up some phrases from the Japanese girls, from TV, and from Michiko, the sweet lady who comes to our house a couple times a week to clean and cook.

I feel important in my navy jumper, white blouse, and navy jacket. We change our outdoor shoes into soft, black loafers in the wood-paneled cloakroom where we must observe the sacred rule of silence and obey the high school girls.

The weight of religion is heavy, and the Sisters are kind but strict. At Mass in the cathedral-like chapel, we wear lace veils to our shoulders and white gloves, and we button up our navy-blue jackets. The strength of the hymns—our voices echoing from the domed ceiling—and the solidarity of little girls and young women gives a sense of mystery if not piety. The ceremony and pomp of Pope John XXIII, the chant, and song hold the most sway for this questioning girl.

Some classmates are daughters of diplomats. South African, Indonesian, Ceylonese, Bulgarian, Dutch, Swedish, Danish, Thai, Indian, Chinese, Canadian, Japanese, and English. We American girls—mostly military—wear our best dresses on family days, while most girls wear their national costumes. They sing and play their instruments and display art and favorite foods. My first taste of strong, black Arabic demitasse coffee is from an Egyptian friend's family booth.

I Must Have Wandered

One sunny June morning in 1962, my mother points and orders me to retrieve the brown Oxfords I carelessly left in my school cubby on the last day of school. I'd worn my soft black uniform loafers on the bus, and she just noticed they weren't in my closet. "Walk to school and get them!"

Obedient if not somewhat daunted by her demand, I leave home, walking briskly along the fieldstone border wall. My hands are empty, and I want to be quick, not thinking that my dad, away on temporary duty, would not have wanted me to make this trip alone, certainly not without my military identification card.

I step outside the gate, past the Japanese guards. I know our school bus uses this gate. They wave "bye," and I emerge onto the Tokyo sidewalk.

On my left is Meiji Jingu and the entrance of the shrine, marked by its tall wooden torii gate. Feeling excited and brave, I merge with commuters near Harajuku station. To my right are the modern buildings of the Shibuya business district, and I rest briefly, leaning against a plate glass department store window to gather a memory of the route. Boys and girls in school uniforms, women in kimonos, and the young and elderly pass me. I bow and smile in greeting. I have to go through the crossroads with the crowd. When safely across the wide intersection, drawn by memory, I trudge up the narrow street in my private school's Hiro neighborhood and turn right under the torii lintel into my school grounds.

Feeling like an imposter, I pick up my pace and jog up the driveway to the main building wearing Keds, a sleeveless shirt, and shorts, feeling self-conscious out of uniform. I climb the stone steps through the main door and enter the front hall, slipping past a few nuns and summer boarders. I stop in the restroom.

No jackets hang in the cloakroom. I squat and pull my culprit shoes from my cubby where I had left them. Relieved, I scurry into the hallway and outdoors to the driveway. Passing the hefty concrete lantern on my left and the silent tea house on my right, I face the play yard, turn right, and walk under the torii.

My heart races. I'm uncertain. *Am I in the wrong place?* I keep walking. Now I'm in a lane outside a souvenir shop where I've been with my parents. *How did I get here?* I have no yen in my pocket.

Out of nowhere, Kathy, my best neighborhood playmate who rides the bus to school with me, and her mother stand in front of me. Kathy smiles. Her mother looks concerned. "How did you get here? Are you alone?"

"My mother made me go to school for my shoes." I hold them up. I detect in myself a slight self-pitying tone and feel confused.

Without comment or delay, Kathy's mom points to her parked American car. "You'll come with us." She puts a coin in the soda dispenser that stands on the sidewalk outside the shop. "Here, a have a drink." She offers me a small open bottle of Pepsi, and I accept it and climb into the back seat. No one speaks as she drives through the rear gate into our complex and pulls into her parking space, which is across the street and a few courts up from ours. "Okay, here we are."

"Thank you! Bye, Kathy!" I hand the empty Pepsi bottle to her, push open the car door, slam it, and run across the street to our unit at the far end of four, clutching my loafers.

"Mom, I'm home! I have my shoes! I saw Kathy and her mom outside the gate shopping, and they brought me home."

She doesn't ask for details, and I don't tell her about my trouble. "Okay. Put them in your closet."

I don't remember anything about the rest of the day.

In the story Dad told me when I was six, everyone but me was lost, and I was taken home by strangers. Perhaps in my deep recesses of self, I would run away and would not— could not—be found. I walked away in a dream. Unseen, I must have wandered. There was no sense of time. I must have lapsed into my orphanhood.

My Poem

In final period study hall, our sixth-grade class occupies the farthest rows, and as one of the tallest, I'm in the last seat near the cupboard. Last period. As one of the tallest, I'm in the last row. Mother Jerome monitors up front with the youngest classes, so a few of us can make a bit of mischief.

I should be reading homework, but I'm writing a long rhyming poem based on "The Shoemaker and the Elves." While checking on the girls at the back, Mother strides over to me. "What are you writing?" Her tone is suspicious.

I proudly hold my carefully crafted verses up to her. "It's a poem!"

She swipes the paper from my hand and, with a sharp glance at its title, returns it. "You did not write this!" She scoffs and turns away.

I murmur, "I did! It is mine!" I'm wounded. So pleased with my work, I expected credit for my descriptive language: "The shoes he made of tightened moss and shined them til they showed a gloss…"

I assume Mother Jerome confiscated my poem—I don't recall seeing it again. When I told my mom about the troubling incident, she said, "You're too sensitive!" and it added insult to injury. Yes, the nun hurt my feelings. I cared that my poem wasn't appreciated. It was never spoken of again. But Mom would repeat the comment about my sensitivity through the years.

Encounter

White mesh veils lie on the wide windowsill at the back of the hall, available to a few of the oldest girls to wear to the chapel. We are considered trustworthy, and we shuffle piously through the upper convent halls in our soft black loafers. A few find the way to enter the choir loft to view the high, ornamented ceiling and overlook the wooden pews, altar, and statues below. That is not for me.

One afternoon, we turn a corner a see a nun kneeling in the middle of a hallway. Her eyes closed, she prostrates herself on the tile floor. We turn and bolt, shocked by what we witness. We twitter about it on the way to study hall and slip through the back door to return our veils.

We girls think we'll be in trouble, but Mother Jerome never mentions our encounter. This has to be forbidden! We return solemnly to our books.

Saints and Sinners

During our second summer in Tokyo, I ride my bicycle to daily Mass at the Washington Heights chapel, and after, I visit the pocket-sized library to pore over stories of mysticism and young holy women who've seen apparitions and witnessed miracles long ago. St. Bernadette and St. Teresa, "The Little Flower," and sweetness and sensitivity appeal to me. Teresa was a Carmelite, and I imagine the tan gummy, the sweetness of candy cubes wrapped in cellophane. She bravely suffered through a fatal illness without complaint. I know I could never suffer without complaining. The image in *Young People's Lives of the Saints* shows her lying perfectly flat on her back in her convent bed. It fascinates me that she seems to lack a body under her blanket.

I read that Maria Goretti was stabbed to death at my age, eleven, by a boy cousin. I don't know what rape means, but I admire her for fighting him, and I'm thinking that girls and women are vulnerable because they are small or weak.

My father is religious and sometimes hurts me. I see that faith doesn't save us from harm. He has said I deserved it. He even has said he could kill me. It frightens me that this could be true. I know it's because he gets migraines and works hard. Once he yelled, "Go to your room with no dinner! Only bread and water!" He enforced it and sent me upstairs with crusts. I was mortified, but I must have deserved it.

I'd been taught that God punishes sin and forgives us if we are sorry. Dad never has said he forgives me. Neither does he say he's sorry, but maybe he apologizes to God. Maybe it's a sin when he hits me. Mom doesn't apologize either, but I have to apologize to them for being bad. I never get a hug of forgiveness, even if I'm contrite.

Cherry trees line the road in Washington Heights, showing off their fluffy pink blossoms. It's our second spring in Tokyo. Maybe I've brought home a report card with a lower grade in arithmetic, or maybe my character development score has slipped. Dad has said his career depends on character reports that stay high. "I always get top ERs." I don't know what this stands for, but it has something to do with excellence. "That's why I get promoted," he says.

Mom has sewn a dirndl box-pleat skirt and tailored jacket in mint green and white check, a pretty, grown-up Easter suit for me. She pinned a rhinestone-jeweled duck on my collar's lapel. Dad has brought home from a TDY—temporary duty overseas—handmade silk cocoon slip-on shoes for me and pumps for Mom, and a matching clutch for me and a handbag for Mom. But he forbids me to wear my new outfit to Easter Sunday Mass because of some offense, and I'm crushed. I can't understand why he denies me what I'd be so happy to wear. As usual, Mom doesn't say a word about it, at least not in front of me, and she must be disappointed too. She puts out an ordinary shirtwaist dress for me on Easter to wear with my usual Sunday shoes. Everyone must see my red eyes and sad face in church.

I'm allowed to wear my Easter outfit next Sunday, but it is little consolation, because it feels like Dad has punished me all over again by adding insult to my injury.

I hate him! I rage to Dear Diary. Since he confiscated my Schaeffer cartridge pen, I gouge the page with the list of my restrictions and punishments in red ballpoint. *I must not talk to Dad. No bicycle riding. No playing with my friend, Kathy. Why does he want me to feel loss?*

He wants me to be grown-up at the table, utensils placed and used correctly, bread sliced in half before I butter it. It's not a joy to be with him at dinner. I'm a pretty mannerly kid, articulate, not uncouth as he says. He demands perfection. He says he loves me sometimes, but I can't measure up to his demands of perfection. Julie is still little, and he wants me to set a good example for her.

Goodbye, Washington Heights

In June 1963, I pass the sixth grade and leave the gates of ISSH for the last time. Dad says, "We have to move to Johnson AFB." He has been there, maybe Mom too. "Washington Heights is going to be torn down this summer to make way for the 1964 Summer Olympics. All these buildings, the houses, and offices will disappear."

I realize he wants to protect us from the sight of the destruction, and besides, he has orders to leave by a certain date. I have a picture in my head of how bad the tear-down will be. Not only will I be leaving my beautiful school and all the girls I've become close to, but our house and my military friends' houses will be destroyed. I tell myself to hold onto my good memories. I have my Swedish friend Ingrid's mailing address near Sacred Heart. Kathy's family will move to California. I have her address, but leaving is always hard.

In June 1962, around the time we arrived in Tokyo, the United States Air Force (USAF) ended its use of Johnson AFB—it had been headquarters of the Fifth USAF headquarters during the occupation—and there was a surge of United States military families throughout Japan.

With the Buick's trunk full, we take a rural ride to the village of Sayama, about an hour north of Washington Heights. On the way, we see farm fields and houses tucked into the countryside. Off in the distance is snow-topped Fuji-san, Mount Fujiyama, rising from the hills. On some days in Tokyo, we caught a glimpse of Fuji-san, but from our new quarters, we'll have a much better view of the heavenly mountain.

I see Johnson Air Station as a huge congested hub of American cargo planes, fighter jets, military vehicles, buses, American cars, office buildings, and uniformed personnel. Hyde Park housing is our home until the summer of 1964: a single-family, one-story cottage in a court of five units with a central grass yard for Julie to play with her little friends. There aren't many good places for me to ride my bike, not like on the wide streets and off-road paths of Washington Heights.

The moist summer brings a variety of insects as it did in Washington Heights, where we had cicadas. Kids cruelly capture praying mantises in delicate bamboo cages and feed them ants we have stunned with a stone. We toss salt on slugs that grip the trees and watch them struggle and writhe. We tie long threads to the rear leg of June bugs, allowing them to fly on tethers. Giant rhinoceros beetles come to our back step, attracted by the porch light, and Mom, always curious about animals, puts bread and jam down for one to nibble on. She is kind to animals, despite her history of euthanizing dogs to suit her convenience.

Seventh grade at coed Johnson Junior High takes my life into a downturn. No uniforms, crowded, noisy classrooms that open onto covered walks, no hallways, no cloakroom, no huge chapel, no sweet girls, no open-air play yard. I realize how lucky I was at ISSH the past two years. My change to junior high is traumatic. At twelve, life feels chaotic and miserable, but I try to get involved in music. I take French horn since I can't have a piano—we didn't bring the one from Washington Heights—and it's bulky to carry the horn on the school bus, adding to my sense of awkwardness. I find out that two neighbor girls sing in the base chapel choir, and I join. I sing every day, and soon I'm playing Armed Forces Radio on my Sony transistor to hear the Top 20.

We girls pile into a military bus to ride to the base gym and change into green, one-piece rompers in a congested locker room. I hate to shower and dress beside girls who are more developed than me. The boys are sarcastic, sometimes cruel, like John S., who stomps on my t-strap's toes. New math is beyond my grasp—impossible. There is no quiet in class. Everyone passes notes. Everything is wrong: my dresses, my awkward body, my permed hair.

Mom and I go to a Japanese-operated beauty shop—a concession on base—before Thanksgiving. The news breaks through the shop radio music. *Kennedy shot!* The ladies hold their hands to their mouths and speak in a shocked tone. Kennedy was elected when we lived in Louisiana. With the military always around me, I worry about Russian nuclear bombs and the fallout that might be in the rain. I'd heard something about "the age of anxiety."

At home we watch Johnson's swearing in and JFK's funeral. I feel sad for Mrs. Kennedy, Caroline, and John-John. We watch wall-to-wall coverage of the motorcade, the president's blood on Jackie's pink suit, Lee Harvey Oswald, and Jack Ruby, all in the Japanese language.

The world has changed. It's become harsh and violent. *What will this mean for me? I must grow up to survive.*

A classmate, a cute boy with blond slicked-back hair, Ronnie Lungar, invites me to my first dance, a sock hop in the spring of 1964. We dance the twist to the jukebox, the Beatles "I Wanna Hold Your Hand," "Please, Please Me," and "She Loves You." It must be love, because Ronnie gives me his ID bracelet. We never go anywhere together again, and I don't remember giving it back. I feel better about myself despite my lanky figure and a few red spots.

For military kids, there is always the inevitable "Where did you come from?" A loaded question for me. I always feel lost and out of place. I am tired of having to be the new kid in school, always moving, always having to catch up in school. I know now my sensitivity is a complication of abandonment and the constant upheaval of my family.

Effaced, Erased

One spring Saturday, Dad announces, "I'm going to clean up your bike. I'll paint it to get rid of these scratches before it goes on the boat back to the States." He lifts it onto the grass and nudges the kickstand down with the toe of his Oxford. He tapes newspaper over the seat and handlebars. I sit on the top step of our front stoop, a safe distance from the incoming spray. He shakes the aerosol can and aims a fan of blue at my six-year-old bike. He shakes it again, the beads clacking in the can, and sprays an even coat over my bike. One stab—a pang of dread, or regret—and I am resigned to the new light-blue finish that deletes the scratches and scrapes.

He stands back, pleased. "What do you think?"

I always try to be polite. Dad enforces this trait, and I have learned to be a people pleaser. "I like it, Dad. Thanks." It's a re-do I didn't ask for. I'm unenthusiastic since it will never be the same. He has wiped out the original white markings. He tears off the protective newspaper and walks my two-wheeler to the street. I've never seen him ride it, but now he takes it for a tight spin in the sun. I smile back at his grin, his plaid shorts, his long white socks and brown shoes. His Saturday clothes. I wonder, *Did you have a bike growing up in New York City?*

Sayonara

During these three years, we were always in touch with my grandparents by letters and small reel-to-reel tapes. I've written the occasional letter to Aunt Rosemary. We're about to end our stay in Japan, where I've felt a little at home yet always aware that I'm American, military, a foreigner. I'm finally homesick.

I wander onto a shaded path past the bushes behind our unit and stand at the top edge of a tea paddy, a field of trimmed tea bushes. Down to my right is Ichiban Village, the airmen's housing. It means "number one." Dad sometimes calls me "number one daughter." I squeeze through a break in the wire fence and pick a few of the spicy leaves. Ninety miles off to my left, snow-capped Mount Fujiyama is suspended from soft clouds. I've seen the picturesque farm fields on our rides through the city of Sayama to Yokota airbase and remember farmers bent in the rows. Fuji-san has become part of my daily view, and it will soon be a world away.

I learn about expressions for sweet memory links such as a song, a familiar food, a childhood toy, a place. Home. *Natsukashii* is the word for that connection. *Wabi-Sabi* is a phrase to describe imperfection, impermanence.

~

Part Eleven

Stateside

June 15, 1964, we fly back to the US, with a stop in Honolulu. On the night flight to our next scheduled stop at Oakland, CA, the pilot's voice comes on to tell us about a situation with the landing gear. He would have to circle the San Francisco Bay, releasing sufficient fuel to land safely, he said calmly. Through the window, I see the dark Bay. I dread that we'll fall into the water, something I hadn't thought of once on either of our flights over the Pacific Ocean. The cabin is hushed, only I ask my mother, "Will we crash?" I sense she is concerned too. We continue to circle the water while time is suspended. The runway lights appear, and the landing seems to be normal. Having flown an untallied number of times as a child, I will never fly easily again.

Back in New Jersey, I learn the term "culture shock." I feel out of place in the town I've loved since childhood. The boys and girls I left three years ago have been growing up at a faster rate than I have, it seems. Overseas life hasn't made me mature faster. Military life sheltered me, and the New York metro influence sets my head spinning.

The principal of Ascension School requires me to take summer school math. I stick out like the unknown I am in the New Milford High cafeteria where the class is held. Bullying girls introduce me to the term "mocked out." They snicker at my striped pastel sheath dress that Nana sewed, my short, home-permed hair, and my white ankle socks and loafers. I cry to Mom, "Please don't make me go back there!"

Maybe eighth grade at Ascension School is as hard for me as for my pubescent classmates, and my well-honed smile helps me feel more comfortable here, but a new sense of awkwardness is holding me back. Once again, I'm the new girl, ultra-self-aware, and conscious of everything around me. The equalizing factor for girls is the royal-blue uniform jumper, white, short-sleeved blouse, blue bow tie, blue-and-white saddle shoes, and white anklets. Boys wear a more grown-up version of a uniform in white shirts, ties, and trousers. No one picks on me here. I quickly develop a crush on Tommy P., who'd rather not have the attention.

As warned by the pamphlet Mom handed me at age eleven, "You're a Young Lady Now," distributed by a leading sanitary napkin company, age thirteen brings my period and a new kind of angst.

Sister Loretta is our large, stern, big-hearted, Irish Dominican nun. She says I'm good at etymology and diagramming, but I'm last in the class in math. In a few months, we'll all be taking entrance exams. I'm destined to go to a Catholic all-girls high school.

I practice piano every day after school so Dad doesn't have to hear my mistakes, since he's tired and often has headaches. My lessons are with Miss Gertrude, as they were in fourth grade. She wouldn't have liked my Germany-trained Japanese piano teacher's flamboyant style or her heavy rings on my keyboard.

Dad works in New York City, and is still in Air Force Intelligence. Dressed in civilian clothes, he walks several blocks to River Road to catch the Red and Tan bus and takes the subway to his office.

Mom and Nana have dinner on the table for me and Julie at 4:30, and they eat with us. Granddaddy rarely eats dinner with the family—Nana feeds him when he's ready. He has retired from his shop and turned the tractor-trailer repair shop over to his son.

Coming through the front door around 6:00, Dad calls "Hi," puts his coat in the closet and goes upstairs. After changing from his city work clothes into something comfortable, he goes down to the kitchen, where Mom scurries to fix him a plate. She sits at the table with him, and they review the mail. When he's finished eating, Dad returns to their bedroom for the evening to read and watch TV with Mom.

On this fall day, Dad drives into work. At about 4:30 p.m., he brings in a rust-and-white puppy, a beagle-terrier type. Mom and Dad love him and name him Sam. They keep him in the kitchen behind a wood baby gate that we all have to step over. His bed is under the wall phone, and his bowls are on the other side of the cabinet with the phone books. He's cute, but I don't really think of him as mine, and he annoys the heck out of me by biting at my slippers. He becomes part of our family, but he could never replace my Rascals. Nana, Mom, and I walk him. I never play with him like Rascals. He was the best.

Facts

"You never do anything with me," I whine.

"What do you *want* me to do?" Dad asks.

"We never go on vacation or to ball games like other families. You never throw a ball with me." *Who am I kidding?* I've left behind kickball, bike riding, dollhouses, and Barbies, so I don't know where that came from.

He goes upstairs. I know he has better things to do with his time.

My best friend, Sue, who lives in the next town, is the daughter of one of the few lay teachers, so she is allowed to attend Ascension School. She must be a few inches shorter than me and has soft, golden-brown hair, thinner than mine. We walk the mile and a half to each other's homes during winter vacation, and our parents drop us off to shop for clothes at Bergen Mall. I'm relieved to have a clothing allowance. I'm tired of Mom's and Nana's sewing styles, a boxier fit than what appeals to me. Sue and I buy our first pairs of bell-bottoms; mine are lined and camel colored. I notice my shape changing with hips and slight breasts. That summer, we are in the woods at the county park, kissing boys we don't know.

After Sunday Mass and bacon and eggs, my father sits in his easy chair and reads *the New York Times.* He gestures for me to sit on the couch. Before I can think, he is talking to me. "You've heard about where babies come from."

It's not a question. My face feels hot, and I look down at my hands.

He mumbles something, much of nothing. I'm tensed up when his voice hitches and brings tears. "You know, Mary Ellen, I'm the reason your mother and I didn't have children."

Oh no! He's going to cry—please don't! I can't stand it! You didn't have children? You have me and Julie, but we're not really yours.

My adoptive father burdens me with his loss and his ego and again confronts me with my questionable origins. His loss smacks me in my brain, but I grieve, too, and he is oblivious to the pain that he contributed to.

I don't have it in me to feel sorry for him. I can't pity him. My compassion for him is rigid. I am so confused and panicked that I want to flee from him, from the house. I feel trapped. If only he could face our relationship straight on with the truth rather than with secrecy and shame. The child of his dreams can't be made legitimate merely by sheltering her, by his adoptive ownership.

His photos portray the adopted daughter. Her smile hides what she feels without the means to articulate it: that she is an imposter, a misfit in this family. At thirteen, the image of perfection is fading.

Behind My Back

My new girlfriends and I walk a few miles back and forth to shop for records at Two-Guys, or we take the bus to E. J. Korvette and Bergen Mall. As young teenagers, we express our new freedom by walking, always alert for boys. Little kids, like Julie, ride small bikes with banana seats. Some older kids have three-speed or ten-speed bicycles. I'd rather avoid the teasing I'm sure I'd get for riding a cruiser with manual brakes.

One fall day, I consider riding it, but it's missing from its spot on its kickstand in the back of the garage. My heart sinks. I run to the kitchen door and call to whoever is there. "Mom! Nana! Where's my bicycle? It's gone!"

"Your father brought it over to Cousin Johnny's," Mom says. She is as matter-of-fact as the time she told me Rascals had been put to sleep.

"Why? Why didn't you tell me?"

"He gave it to Johnny for the kids. You weren't using it anymore." Mom is never apologetic.

He gave my bicycle to my cousins without talking to me about it. *Behind my back!* He had just painted it for me. We never spoke of it. I feel cheated. I hide my adopted adolescent girl's tears in the garage. My heart aches, and at the same time I feel betrayed and furious at all of them. Wasn't I entitled to at least be asked if I minded giving a piece of my life away? Dad never said a thing about it before or after. It was like my bike had never existed. Just like everything else I had lost.

Our Buick was the cousin's car now too. I wasn't in on that either and had no warning, but we were getting new cars: a Falcon for Nana and a Wildcat for Mom. The green Buick was in my life since the start. We'd taken it north and south all those years. It had rumbled on the narrow streets of Tokyo. It was as least a part of my world as my blue bicycle. All we had was Dad's to do with as he saw fit.

Part Twelve

War Time: The Teens

I connected with Chris Kelly from our first day at Academy of the Holy Angels (AHA) in September 1965, and we would stay friends for life. Taller than me at five foot nine and lanky, she had pale, fine features. She lived all her life in the same house in Westwood, two towns north of ours. She'd been through one elementary parochial school. The youngest of five grown children, Chris was the only one at home with her mother. Her father, a shipping executive, lived in Saint Louis. I never learned how long her parents had been separated, but I knew that he died of cancer while we were in high school. It seemed unusual to me that she never spoke about him, but I didn't talk much about my father either. I met her mother several times—a tall, attractive woman and a smoker, like Chris would eventually become. She had a quiet wit about her and a good smile like her daughter. She called my friend Christina.

We rode the school bus together and knew how to put each other in hysterics laughing. Behind the nuns' backs, we cut up and snuck notes. As sophomores, we became bolder, and I often took the heat for behavior. Chris set an example of how to dress out of school. She shopped for the best fashions. A straight, navy-blue coat with mod epaulets and brass buttons was *au courant*, and I had to have one like hers. Her height and weight made it gorgeous on her, and her make-up and hair were more interesting than how I saw mine.

Music connected us to our other classmates Judy and Karla, with Bob Dylan and Joan Baez with folk guitar. Chris liked the Rolling Stones and Beatles, as her older brother did. I noticed we were assuming a harder, rebellious attitude with these new friends who went to the West and East Village to see bands and solo players. All of us were bright, with academic potential. I learned to smoke pot in town with kids who had graduated from grade school with me and their extended family of friends. Some girls in my school were wearing leather sandals and ponchos and changing into their school loafers and bobby socks. We rolled our pleated plaid skirts up above our knees. We were in various stages of boy craziness, and some of us were preoccupied with the goings-on outside our academy.

In 1966 and 1967, a boy named Frank made the county paper for his suspension and lawsuit over his right to wear his hair long. We girls thought of it as a Beatle cut and loved his shaggy, mop-top look. When Chris brought the newspaper clippings to sophomore class, it caused a stir.

Most girls in our group of friends managed to keep their grades up. I continued to falter in math. Algebra II and geometry summer school classes were inevitable. The classes were held in a neighboring town's high school, so I walked both ways, about four miles total. I became friendly the second summer with a girl whose boyfriend picked her up in a hot car after class. He drove us around with "Wild Thing" playing loudly. I didn't let them drop me off in front of my house.

The nuns reported to my parents that I was spending too much time with Chris. Once Dad heard she was thought a bad influence on me, my days at AHA soured. I couldn't keep away from my fashionable, flamboyant best friend. She was going to be a journalist, she said. She was artistic, witty, smart, funny, and had goals. We continued our laughter, and she kept up her grades. She lifted my spirits, and I got into trouble. I refused to give up my friends, not after all the ones I had lost to moving.

I told my mother so. "You can't stop me from being her friend! I like her a lot!"

When our town high school made the paper, I began to think about transferring. I knew of a couple of the boys who were suspended for refusing to get their haircut. *How exciting! How dangerous! Rebels, like me!* They played guitars and sang in a group that played at Catholic Youth Organization (CYO) and high school dances.

I took every opportunity to be out of the house when my father was at work. I hung out at the homes of kids who were in public high instead of walking directly home from the bus stop. I got off the bus at 3:30, and Dad didn't get in until 5:30. I could squeeze in an hour of relaxation with music and friends. We played records and sang in harmony, often with a guitar or two. My new friend Bob's mom and dad were separated, and he lived with his dad and elder brother. His dad was a traveling salesman, and I rarely saw him. I felt sorry for Bob because he had to cook for himself, but I thought it was neat that there were no parents to ask prying questions. I did learn his father yelled at him when he got home from road trips.

Mom warned that I shouldn't walk Sam there, but I headed directly to the block where several friends lived. Looping the leash on the screen door handle at Bob's, or another friend's house, I'd go in for a quick visit, my watch always on my wrist. One day, Dad drove by slowly to confirm his and Mom's suspicions that I had friends I shouldn't have been with. He shouted at me from the car as I stepped outside. "Get home!" I un-looped Sam's leash from Bob's side entrance screen door handle, and adrenalin pumping, walked home, dreading what awaited me. This time it was a restriction. "Never go back there! You're not to go there again!"

How will I get away with going next time? How can I visit my friends without Dad knowing?

One school night during sophomore year, my father pushed my bedroom door open. Mom had been letting me keep it shut. He burst in, shouting and striding toward me, where I sat at my vanity. I leaned back, and he yanked open the little drawer and rifled around with his stubby fingers. *He's done this before!* He snapped up a scrap of paper like he knew it was there. It was nothing more than a penciled fragment of song lyrics by Herman's Hermits, "No Milk Today." I was astonished that he accused me of referring to drugs. He said, "This is a code!" He said I was planning to pass it to a schoolmate to make a drug pickup.

"No! That's not true! It's only a song! It's nothing!"

"You are damaging my security clearance!"

I thought he was crazy, but I was terrified. He had the power. I had no idea what he was talking about and dreaded what was to come. He slapped me. I denied and cowered. He yanked my hair. He drew his leather belt from his pants and hit the back of my legs, arms, and shoulders.

I was nearly his height at five foot seven, so he had to put out more effort. My acid tears burned, my face disfigured by howls. I heaved choking sobs as he raged and rummaged through my dresser drawers. He demeaned me. He violated my privacy.

When it was over, he sat on my bed and quieted himself. "Go wash your face with a washcloth."

As if he, what, wanted to nurture me? I hated him more than ever. He stayed behind, and I stumbled to the adjacent bathroom. My back and arms hurt. I heard him scramble around in my closet. *What is he looking for?* I buried my shame in the washcloth's cold composure. Our tenuous bond dissolved down the drain.

Wandering from the Truth

Our family's nomadic lifestyle came to an end when we returned from Japan. I know my mother was happiest home in New Jersey with her mother, who was her best friend, and I realized their roles never changed. Mom always took Nana's guidance—she stayed her little girl.

Their conversations often took place around and over what I wanted to say. In Nana's greater wisdom, she usually left the room to give us the space to talk. Mom didn't know how to pick up the cues, and there was rarely an exchange of any importance. She was miles away while I rambled.

I recall feeling ungrounded, confused about where I and Julie came from and how our family was related. Oh, I understood we were adopted, but it didn't stop me from wondering *who I was.* My identity confusion heightened as my parents seemed to slough me off like an excess skin. I wanted them to talk with me but couldn't ask questions for fear it would upset them. To make matters worse, Mom was given to saying versions of "I don't understand you!" "Why can't you be like me?" and "You're completely different from me!"

Why? Why can't I be like you? Why do I feel lost? Why does something feel missing? Why do I feel different from other kids? Why don't I fit in? What are my secrets? What are your secrets? Why do I have to lie?

Why tell the truth when a lie was boosted like adrenaline? When I could see my friends without my parents knowing? When my imagination could conjure excitement? I sometimes delivered my stories to her back at the kitchen sink. When they fell flat, when she had no time, was impatient, or her mind was elsewhere, she listened to a story that sparkled with childish innocence. The little girl in me she once knew. I told her lies to please her, to impress, to disguise, to seem innocent, or perhaps to protect myself from punishment. Why tell her where I was going? If she did ask, my answer may or may not have been a lie.

Is my lying an adoption defect? How many lies have you told me?

I was straying. I was flailing. In the summer of age fifteen, I was out of the house as much as possible. I formed a defiant boundary, a line of demarcation against family life. Since I was powerless to fix the bond, I steeled myself with lies. I didn't understand then that our family's transience and my father's frequent separations inhibited our emotional connection. I was in full rebellion. In time, my facile and frequent fabrications were transparent to Mom.

Letter to the Psychiatrist: What I'd Write Today

Dear Dr. W.,

You were the tall and slender, quiet, gray-haired gent who sat behind the massive desk. You directed me, a shy, fearful sixteen-year-old girl, to sit in the uphol-

stered chair a distance across from you. You may recall that my adoptive mother was a public health supervisor with the hospital where you were on staff.

It came to a head one evening at dinner. I was trapped in a lie, my father jumped up from the table, and my stomach sank with dread when he raged at me. "You're a pathological liar! We're taking you to a psychologist!" I was unaware that my mother had tipped him off about my casual lies and made the appointment with you.

Doctor, you must have seen me stiffen in defense as you took notes. You dozed during my tense responses. You'd heard it all before: the adolescent angst, the vague answers to "why do you lie?" I feared what would happen to me if you found I was a psychopath. Would you tell my parents? I feared their power. Would I be sent away to a home for ungrateful, adopted liars? You didn't ask me how I shaped my lies in my struggle to recover my identity.

At the family meeting, I exploded in tears early. I used the moment to rage against them. I can't recall my defense for lying, but I expressed my sense of injustice for their privacy invasions and physical abuse. I saw the shock, maybe embarrassment, on their faces, and Dad cut the session short.

"You won't be going back there! I'm not spending ninety dollars a session for that kind of abuse!" Dad shouted in the car. There were no family meetings at home. I cried all the way home that evening.

Dad told me, "Sit in that chair! Ungrateful wretch!" What is a wretch but a contemptible person? They loved me according to my reciprocation, which I

*couldn't fully give. I couldn't truly love them. I some-
times liked them, but I couldn't give them what they
wanted, which was obeisance and humble gratitude.
Their love was conditional. I couldn't mirror them.
Emulate them. I believe now that they grieved a ghost
child they couldn't have and mourned the child I was
not. My need was to assert my place in the family and
distance myself from parents who were not my own. I
mourned the child I might have been had I not been
relinquished by my birth mother. They pushed me to
replace what was lost to their infertility.*

*Yes, my parents gave me every material thing I
needed. I was not an ingrate, yet it never occurred
to me to say the words, "Thank you for this special
life you gave me, this life you chose for me." Do any
teenagers?*

*It upset me when Dad accused me of changing my
demeanor as soon as I got what I wanted from them.
My attitude changed. "You are pleasant until you get
what you want from us. Then you turn and become
sour." I wasn't aware of this attitude, but being angry
at me didn't help me. It didn't "correct" me. It made
me feel worse about myself rather than want them
more. They didn't understand how much I had lost
to abandonment and adoption: my identity, family
heritage, and birth records.*

*Doctor, did you reassure them that, after more
sessions, I could be helped? How much help did this
troubled, pained adopted child need? Perhaps you said
I'd outgrow the lying. Did you give my parents literature
about adoption? Recommend books? The legal system
of adoption was built on lies. I was lied to, yet was*

expected to be honest. The soul of me had been crying to know "the real me," my authentic self. How would you have resolved our therapy had I been allowed to continue? Might you have said that knowledge of my genetic identity would be healthy? Might you have agreed there was a psychological and medical need to know? Might you have volunteered to assist us? It was the 1960s, and the seal of adoption was firmly affixed.

My adoption was one of myriad in the industry of abandoned and transferred children in the postwar era. My Catholic Air Force parents were perceived as privileged, well fit to provide opportunities that my unwed mother could not. Perhaps it wasn't of concern to the adoption agency that military transience and disruption would deal upset to the relinquished newborn, since there wasn't the sense of newborn adoption loss we now understand. Their system was ready to place white foundlings in white, middle-class homes. Yet we packed and settled, packed again, and moved again.

However well balanced by genetics—how good natured and smiling—I believe a relinquished infant feels the loss that results in identity confusion.

My psyche was both inherited and imprinted on. I was a duality. Uprooted repeatedly within my military family, troubles sprouted by degrees in the growing awareness that mystified both me and them. I remained a misfit, holding onto a vague fantasy: the ghost of another family.

Did I hold in my psyche, in my young mind, that I was rescued like an abandoned puppy at the roadside? A florid tale of love and sacrifice? What of survivor

guilt? A couple's faith and frustration shaped my
identity, but my genes and psyche knew. All I could
do was to try to make sense of the early switch. My
parents made a family, if not by blood, but I felt I
couldn't measure up. That's why I learned to expand
my story, Doctor.

Yours truly,
Mary Ellen C.

I read this blog post in my forties, and it still rings true.
I'm struck by the similarities to my mother and her difficulty coping with an adopted child, especially a daughter
whose physical attributes and temperament were so different from hers.

Excerpted from Adoptee BlogSpot (no longer active)

"The intolerant adoptive mother…the disappointed
adoptive parent that feels the need and is compelled
to verbally destroy the adopted child's character, self-
esteem and cripple the adopted child's self-aware-
ness…The adoptive mother's disapproving voice,
resentment toward the adopted child, and the adop-
tive mother's favorite habit is the constant picking
apart of the adopted child's failures in life and focus
on the child's failure to be the ideal adopted child…
therefore being adopted and not the parent's blood
offspring is the exact problem in the parent-child
relationship and the reason for the predictable non-
offspring child abuse…even in a case where there is no
biological child–this may be due to resentment over
the non-biological adopted child relationship. The

constant verbal attacks are an unconscious activity to remind the adopted child of their outcast, non-biological status...The adopted child that is "Acting Out" is the most psychologically healthy, resilient, and self-preservation motivated..."

Lost My Way

The tension between my parents and me heightened with no apparent solution to my full-on adopted adolescent identity crisis. Each of us struggled to maintain ground. In the early winter of 1967, in my junior year, Dad was assigned to a year in northern Thailand. It was the height of the Southeast Asian wars. The moment he was gone, I pushed my mother in earnest, using dramatic, tearful pleas to take me out of the girls' academy. I begged her to let me transfer to New Milford High School (NMHS), the same place I was bullied the summer we returned to the States.

The all-girls academy in Tokyo in fifth and sixth grades was challenging socially, but I loved the girls of many cultures and smiles. At Holy Angels, I was dying to get around boys, although I couldn't say this, of course, as the reason to transfer. "I'll go crazy if I have to stay in that place!"

After January midterms, I began classes at NMHS in the graduating class of 1969. I felt my way around eleventh-grade schedules. It was the first time since Johnson Junior High that I had male teachers. I put on a smile and bumped into kids I recognized from Catholic grammar school but knew few in a student body of close to five hundred. The multifloor high school was a maze of floors and classrooms, so different from the modern architecture of the brand-new school I'd left behind. I went through the motions like a stranger, an alien among young adults, many of whom had known each other all through school. I tried to act as cool and confident as they did but couldn't be anyone but myself: friendly, eager to please, somehow different. Lost.

We girls were not yet allowed to wear pants to school but could wear our dresses and skirts way above the knee. I'd been getting a clothing allowance for a couple of years. Shifts, cute vested suits, miniskirts, and dresses, fishnet and opaque tights, stacked heels, and Nehru shirts with embroidery down the front—I loved the mod look and freedom of expressing the taste that Christina guided me toward.

I still met with Chris—she had a white Corvair and let me practice driving in a parking lot. We shopped at Bergen Mall, Garden State Plaza, Bloomingdale's, Army Navy Prozy's in Hackensack, and the Florence Shop, and Mandee's in Bergenfield. We wore hip-hugger bell-bottoms, pea jackets, and ribbed Henley pullovers. We lightened our hair and had it bobbed and layered. We painted our eyes like Twiggy with brown lower lashes and wore white, icy-pale blue, pink Yardley, or Mary Quant lipstick. When I got more involved with my new high school crowd, I didn't see my best friend for a few years.

I was in college prep classes, but I had no clear aspirations and no guidance. I flirted with failure, in danger of falling through the cracks. I don't recall Mom asking how I was doing in school. She probably knew the answer.

Why had I subjected myself to the stressful transfer? My science teacher at Holy Angels implored me not to make the move. The frequent moves of military life had added to my sense of rootlessness. She said it would be best to stay put. Unconsciously, I followed my father's lead by transferring midyear. Was I trying to take control? Did I reckon myself capable of making an important decision like this on my own, or was it a sign of desperate need? A constant ache. This sad and lonely girl did not make the right choices. Not that my new school was substandard. On the contrary, academic achievement was high in my new school, but because I was unguided at home and at school, there was nothing good for me in the change. No one was going to save me from a failed attempt at being independent. I felt guilty for leaving Catholic school without my father's consent. I felt sneaky. Mom facilitated the transfer because she was at her wits' end with me. It was a risky move, one of many risks I'd begun to take, and my dad couldn't stop me.

Julie was in kindergarten at Ascension School, and Nana shuttled her and cared for her as she had for me all those years ago. Mom was a public health nurse again—back in the workforce after almost twenty years, a supervisor of visiting nurses at Englewood Hospital. She connected me with a job in the clinic when I was sixteen: a summer replacement for the permanent registrar, Mrs. Kruse. It was good for me to be off the streets those summer days. After work, I couldn't wait to meet my friends.

I wandered town with a loose band of hippies and longhairs—peaceniks, some called us—a counterculture crowd that wanted no part of the Vietnam War. We wore bohemian clothes like fringed buckskin moccasins; hip-hugger bell-bottoms in blue denim, stripes, and solids; balloon-sleeved poet shirts; and peace sign jewelry. Weed was readily available. My boyfriend was on hard drugs. As I rounded the last bend in adolescence, I skidded to a halt.

We squeezed into Debbie's Luncheonette every school day for morning coffee and buttered rolls, cigarettes, chatter, and music on the Wurlitzer. "Sunshine of Your Love," "Nights in White Satin," "Here Comes the Sun," "Hello, I Love You." Kids seemed to like me or were at least interested or curious about me. Not like they were interested in some girls but were friendly toward me, and I felt less lonely. I was starting to fit into a niche, a crowd of kids who got high and listened to tunes.

Some kids knew I'd transferred from Catholic school, that my family was Air Force, and that we always moved. They noticed I was different, sheltered, sometimes restrained, and often restricted. I tried hard to be fun, to be included among any kids who were receptive to me. They called me a "worry wart," and knew that my father sometimes hit me. I rewarded anyone's warmth in kind. I liked sympathy but wasn't sure why. I told only my closest friends that I was adopted, and I can't recall what they thought of it. I knew of no other adopted kids.

I fit each situation like a chameleon. When I thought it mattered, I acted cool—even tough, in charge—with darker makeup and a boyish look. In this way, I took control of social situations. If I used my quirky sense of humor, such as a clownish performance with a close friend named Michael, who was artistic and dramatic, it always got us noticed, the same way it did with Christina at the academy.

For drama club, a group of us worked on an off-beat skit to Blind Faith's "Crossroads." I performed a mime solo in front of the rock band before a full school day auditorium. How I did that, I'm not sure. It was pure excitement and adrenalin. I was the same girl who performed lead roles in school plays at Sacred Heart. Chorus was the brightest part of the week. Music was always my salvation.

I did well in English and vocabulary. Introspective verse tumbled out of me into a spiral notebook in study hall. There was no end to my fierce loneliness, and no matter how well I may have been loved, I felt hollow. My mind was in chaos.

Aloneness

It hurts to be alone and not know who you are or
where you're going
To have no one to pick up your cause or show you
the way.
And the worst part of being alone is to love and not
be loved in return.

Dancing was cathartic. The winter mixers and summer block dances were packed, and we attended any we could get to if boys we knew played. Under green, pulsing lights in a church basement coffee shop, on the concrete behind the borough hall, at CYO and high school gym dances. My dress was refined when Dad drove me. When he was not around, I celebrated my new wickedness, my strange alienation. My somewhat sloppier appearance came along with the pot, cigarettes, and beer. My bell-bottom jeans were frayed and ragged and my sweatshirt deliberately inside out, my hair untrimmed. I was a ragamuffin with a boyfriend, and we were high all the time. I was discombobulated, disoriented. My mother was blind to my drug use and sexual behavior while Dad was gone. It was sheer luck I didn't get pregnant.

My mood swings shocked Mom and freaked me out. She witnessed me punch a hole in the drywall of my bedroom. My frustration was out of kilter. *Am I learning anger from Dad? What is going on in my head?* Years ago, I'd kicked the bicycle light-buzzer contraption he had just installed, but I never was destructive with my fine dolls and toys. I remembered the beating I'd taken from Dad in sophomore year and the trouble with lying. I anticipated more trouble when he'd returned, and concealed the gaping hole in the drywall with a full-page magazine photo of John Lennon wearing granny glasses—my rebel hero.

When Dad came home from Southeast Asia, his heart was heavy from the horrors. We had seen some of it on TV and now heard snippets from him of his pilots' debriefing. His anguish was devastating. I couldn't reach out to him when I saw his tears, I was powerless to console or hug him, couldn't bring myself to say, "It's okay, Dad, you're home safe and secure with us now." I didn't know how to show him affection, or if any remained. Mom must have understood the depth of his sadness, but I was at a loss, as when I was thirteen, when he wept in front of me.

"I'm giving it up, going to retire now in protest," he said.

Did he feel the same way we did, that it was an unjust war? The war had brought him grief too. I never protested in Washington as some in town had. We hated what Washington and the war were doing to our country. A boy we knew fought and didn't make it home. Classmates would soon enlist or be called up. The draft wouldn't end until December 7, 1972. Dad was leaving the service, and I couldn't wait to leave his home.

That winter, I was suspended for three days when a classmate concealed a plastic bag of pot in my locker. I was that gullible and needy to share my locker with him, to be taken advantage of that way. I'm sure our English teacher had had his eye on the arrangement and reported us to the police. The immediate result was a hasty over-night to Boston, Dad's panicked evacuation with me. During most of the rainy trip, he questioned me like a lawyer. Satisfied with my story, he eventually relaxed and took me to visit Emerson College. But, I'd only taken my PSAT. Direction and motivation were absent, it was too late to apply, and I was not offered an alternative. I'd had a close brush with the law, had gotten myself in a fix—stuck with no plans.

Perhaps he thought he'd fallen short of his duty to the family by leaving that critical year. Did he think he'd failed us? No one had kept me safe. Mom couldn't keep me in AHA. Her strength in childrearing had always depended on his.

In spring of 1969, I was hanging out on the swings behind the borough hall with a small group of friends. Someone's portable radio played "Jumpin' Jack Flash," "Hurdy Gurdy Man," and "Angel of the Morning."

"Uh oh, Mary Ellen, it's your father," a friend said in an ominous, low voice. There was Dad's Buick Wildcat slowing onto the gravel. I had no idea how he knew I was there or that he knew about the little league field. He had no involvement in the town or the youth, let alone that I went there with friends. Perhaps one of his town informants tipped him off; he had at least one in the New Milford Police Department.

"Mary Ellen!" my dad said in a low, menacing voice. "Get in!"

Not a word was said in the car. My heart sank with the dead weight of dread. Within moments, he chased me upstairs to my room. He hit with an open hand with loath-ing fury, frustration, and contempt. All his suspicions and mistrust. He pulled off his belt and used it on me. His blood must have been at a boil. He let the leather fly for my most grievous faults, all my offenses.

I vowed to myself this would be the last time he would hurt me. When he left the room, I stayed there in my fear, sobbing. Mom appeared in the room—she must have wanted to check to see if I was badly hurt, something I'd never seen her do. Within an inch of my life? He'd said it before: "If I don't kill you first!"

I heard him garbling and weeping from my bedroom window. He was in the backyard on a lawn chair, drinking a bottled beer. I was stunned at what I saw. "Mom, what is going on? He's crying and drinking. He never does that!"

She fidgeted and looked away. "He's not right," she said in a low tone, almost apologetically.

He's out of it. From the war? Did he take it out on me? Has Mom worried him about me? Does she feel guilty about it, that she never stopped him from going after me?

There was one last time he physically hurt me. He drove by a friend's house where I sat on the steps with a few friends. "Get home, now!" he yelled. He drove off and waited for me, fuming in the living room. "Slut!" was all he said as he took off his shoe and hit me with the hard heel of his Oxford on my back and legs. I protected my head from his blows. I yelled like I was being killed.

Dad didn't come to my graduation with Mom and Nana. He had given up on me and hadn't recognized my year and a half in NMHS. It was my choice to transfer, not his. I knew I would never consult with him. In fact I never had.

I thought about the time when I was twelve when he turned sharply to me and said, "If you don't improve, I'm going to leave and join a monastery!" The threat caused me to believe it could be imminent. He would leave us to be a monk in Asia. What would Mom, Julie, and I do if he didn't come back? He must have regretted leaving the seminary. Could he no longer bear being with us? With me? Did he want to be a recluse? His resentment and disappointment rippled through our lives. Dad and I were lost to each other. I was a reed in the wind.

I announced that I wouldn't be going back to church. His response was, "Lord have mercy on your soul."

Agnes in High School, NYC

On the roof at 58th St., taken by Agnes's mother.
Engaged—before the War. Agnes in Visiting Nurse uniform.

March 1952, with Al and Agnes, after six months'
separation from my birth mother.

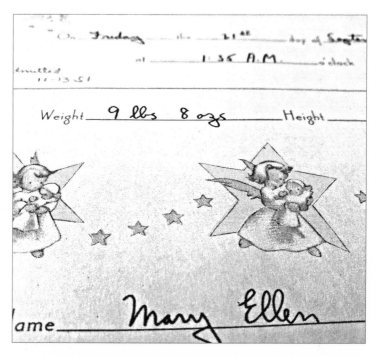

Baby Book fragment—the details.
"Admitted" might mean to a ward at St. Philip's Hospital, or to
the foundling home on the second floor of the Annex before its
renovation in 1952. Where were the babies during
the Children's Annex renovation?

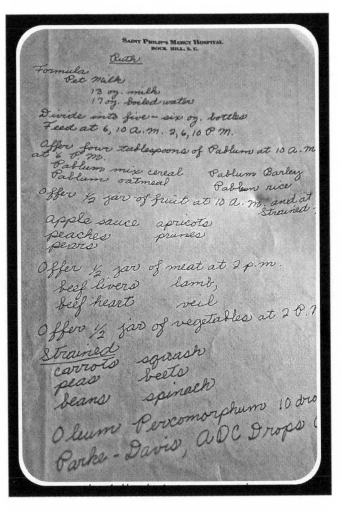

Agnes's feeding instructions from the baby nurse.

Early photos from South Carolina,
including St. Philip's Children's Annex, 1952.

July 1952, NYC.

On Nana's roof with Dobbin, Nov. 1952.

I MUST HAVE WANDERED

Spring and summer; at age three, with Mom in Central Park
on Easter; Mom and Aunt Rosemary in front of the
new home before we moved to New Jersey.

*With Nana; clockwise, top left at a NYC 57th Street store;
with Granddaddy at Aunt Mabel's PA dairy farm she holds
up the fish he and I caught; first day of kindergarten in blue
Ascension School uniform in our back yard in New Milford;
kindergarten graduate, front of home.*

Ages 6–9. Clockwise from top left: at Dennis Street,
Alexandria, Louisiana with Rascals; Texas with Betsy Wetsy
recovering from measles in May 1957; Communion portrait, TX;
same summer, New Milford with Nana's roses; TX first grade;
TX after Dad returned from Tokyo; with Nana, during my time
in NJ, second half of fourth grade at Ascension; another with
Rascals at Dennis St., fully equipped with a six-shooter, hat, and
chaps to play with the neighborhood boys; and with Dad in
Our Lady of Victory churchyard, TX.

Janet's tutu was blue, and mine was pink.
Taken in my backyard.

September 1957, with new bicycle and neighbor, TX.

Fragments of my fifth grade year book ISSH, Tokyo.
Funny, after all these years I remember my classmates' names.
Top left clockwise: Class photo taken outdoors. I am in the
second row from top, the laughing girl second from right. In line
coming back from the recreation yard. I'm in the pom-pom hat,
behind another American girl, Debbie Woods, as I recall; playing
a game--maybe Flags, pigtailed me; study hall last period Junior
School 1st to 5th grades. I'm all the way in the back near the
cupboard in this fragment, probably making mischief with my
classmates. It was from here that some of us would
go to Chapel wearing a shoulder-length veil.

Mary Ellen Gambutti

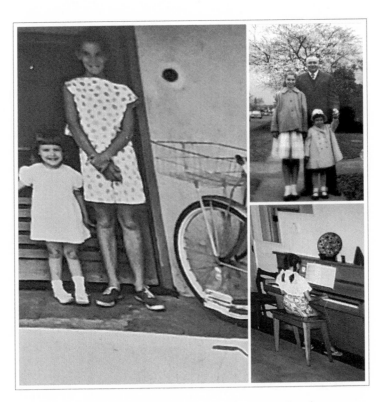

*Tokyo Washington Heights front porch, Easter Sunday—not
wearing the suit Mom sewed; daily piano practice.*

In red Granny dress, August 1966, Atlantic Highlands Air Base at Sandy Hook shore—our only vacation. At the barracks— mosquito infested family bunkrooms, shared bath and shower rooms, and no AC. Here's an article about the history of the base. How it appealed to Dad as a vacation spot, I can only imagine. https://photorecon.net/the-missiles-of-sandy-hook-part-2/

Nana captured me in the brown and white organdy dress she sewed, and "Twiggy" eye lashes.

Finding Leila—Karen, Lawrence Cox and his sister, Helen. My birthmother Leila Grace Cox. Leila's note in the card with a sad looking dog she sent to me in PA after our first meeting.

Karen and Lottie in 2021, Charleston, SC.

Agnes Caffrey, the only Mom I had. Nursing care,
Moravian Hall Square, Nazareth, PA, December 2018.

Mary Ellen Gambutti

My Thrasher siblings Carol and Teri at top. George, Carol, Teri center. Bottom, sister Elizabeth (Libby) Sid Dowis, our paternal grandparents, and our biological father, Andrew Larkin Thrasher Jr.

I MUST HAVE WANDERED   161

Part Thirteen

Ghosts and Panic

"Too dangerous to be allowed into consciousness, they are consigned to a spectral place I call the Ghost Kingdom."

—Betty Jean Lifton, PhD

Adoptees mourn both tangible and intangible losses, I've learned, like the baby who was left behind, the loss of the mother who disappeared, or again when she dies, whether or not we find her. We grieve the persons we might have been had we not been relinquished and the siblings we might have known. All of it matters to adoptees.

I've dreamed of phantoms—others. *I am here. Where are you?* None of my adoptive family members are like me in face or feature. I tell my playground friends, "They aren't my real parents. I have another mother." *Not this mother. Another one.* I hear myself tell them, and as I do, I deepen my thoughts. I ruminate, through this filter of myth, miracle, and mystery, a notion that I appeared from nowhere.

In my teens, I would daydream that a sister or a brother—*real* family—would pass me in a department store, and we would recognize each other. In Sears, by the popcorn machine, I see a girl who looks like me. I stare at her. I look away. *Does she recognize me? Does anyone see me?*

"...This trauma and the severing of the individual from his racial antecedents lie at the core of what is peculiar to the psychology of the adopted child. The adopted child presents all the complications in social and emotional development seen in the own child. But the ego of the adopted child, in addition to all the normal demands made upon it, is called upon to compensate for the wound left by the loss of the biological mother. Later on this appears as an unknown void, separating the adopted child from his fellows whose blood ties bind them to the past as well as to the future."

—Florence Clothier, 1943, "The Psychology of the Adopted Child." Clothier was a psychiatrist at the New England Home for Little Wanderers from 1932 to 1957.

Fear and Dread

An insidious thread of anxiety ran through me since childhood. From age sixteen, pot, beer, uppers, downers, speed, and acid compounded the hypervigilance and messed with my cortisol and mental health. A strong startle reflex is thought to be caused by how a baby is handled and her changes in caretakers. My fear of heights, objects of massive scale, and hypersensitivity might be traceable to newborn trauma, separation, and heredity, as well as to intimidation by my authoritarian father.

"Children should be seen and not heard," from a Middle English proverb, originally referred to women. The adage meant that we shouldn't speak out of turn. Under the watchful eye of adults, we should keep quiet. Don't ask too many questions. Don't ask why. Don't look for meaning. It was a repressive, authoritarian device to control women and children.

Whistling or anything that annoyed Dad—he needed quiet. His strict view, with the notion it would hasten grown-up behavior, was after the old dictum, "Spare the rod and spoil the child." Children wouldn't learn good behavior unless they were physically punished. "Don't make me take off my belt! You'll get the back of my hand across your face, or I'll use the strap on you! You'll get what's coming to you! You are asking for it!" All were viable threats. Mom used "I'll smash you! You'll get a licking! I'll take down the flyswatter!" I wished these people who weren't mine would leave me alone.

At eight and nine, around the time Julie joined our family, my fear of Dad's headaches and corporal punishment caused more anxiety. I had panic attacks at night. I trembled until I made myself throw up. I picked and bit my cuticles until they became infected. My mother also had the habit of picking her skin. I had stomachaches, especially when I was doing homework. I feared illness and dying, perhaps learned from Mom's knowledge of medical terms and diseases that she used around me. She called me a hypochondriac. *Too sensitive!*

Where are you now, Dad? Only once, that I recall, did we talk on the phone when he was away on TDY. He could be gone away for weeks, months, and—three times—for a year. I was forever losing people and places, just as I had lost my birth mother, my original family. With each new school or new state, I made and lost friends. I had to be brave, as that's what military dependents did. It was my duty like it was my mom's. My parents made sacrifices, and so must I. Even Nana had to keep the home fires burning when we were away.

In 1962, in Tokyo, Dad was home with me and Julie while Mom was on an officers' wives' club cruise to Hong Kong. In bed, I heard a whisper, a waking nightmare, a frightening trick of the mind that grew insistent. The voice in my head said, *Faster, faster!* A raspy voice I heard was male. Deeper and deeper I felt sucked in, into my mind, and I couldn't get out.

In my skinny eleven-year-old body, I ran to find Dad reading in their upstairs bedroom. He let me get up on his lap, and I whined about my waking nightmare.

"It's nothing. You're growing up. Go back to bed." My parents rarely took anything I said seriously.

At sixteen, it came back like a trance, like a fog, from nowhere. The ghost voice found its way in as my mind went in deeper. Wearing bell-bottom jeans, supine on my orange bedspread, I stared, mesmerized, at the knotty pine dormer above me.

Faster, faster! It croaked in my ears, in my head, and once evoked, the voice was out of control. I was terrified but couldn't yell for help. I was too old for that. Something wasn't right—I knew it—but I didn't want Mom to know.

When it passed, I sat up and pulled on my lace-up moccasins and left the house for neighborhood streets. I walked to Brookchester strip mall, where other young people where hanging out, loitering, just waiting. Some I knew, and some were strangers. Some older than me, some younger. We had in common at least one thing: we wanted to escape our homes, authority, and responsibilities. We got into cars to escape and smoke cigarettes and pot. We drove to other towns, other neighborhoods. Drank beer, listened to music constantly. New friends in New York apartments, crashed out. Avoided the cops. Thinking we were in charge, in control, daring each other, and fooling ourselves. Not facing the danger.

I was a nineteen-year-old newlywed when panic struck in the little neighborhood grocery store in a hilly town near the Hudson. It set off months of agoraphobia—fear of the marketplace—and years of depression and anxiety, low-level obsessive-compulsive behavior, and low self-esteem that recurred into my thirties.

The self-destructive habits that fueled my mental illness would contribute to the destruction of my young marriage. If only the crisis had been treated. I understood the preciousness of the gift who was there, right in front of me. My mirror image. My beautiful daughter was six years old when I walked out. Left the apartment. I might have thought it through with counseling. I might have listened to someone, might have understood the consequences of acting through my primal wound, and how it would hurt my child. The pain was unspeakable.

At the same time, my adoptive parents were leaving me for California. Selling our permanent home.

The Original Trauma

I was happily married to Phil in 1983 and working in health-related marketing. One night, as I was drifting off to sleep, the swirling brain recurred after years of absence. It was the same hypnotic urgency of *faster* as I went deeper into a swirl of mind. During these episodes, my husband held me until my uncontrollable muscle tremors subsided.

One scorching suburban Philadelphia summer in the late eighties, when I was a personal gardener, my heart began to race while pruning and weeding in a client's yard. I went up to the elderly couple's door for assistance. "I feel dizzy and weak," I said. Maybe it was heatstroke. I was panicking. Her husband was a retired doctor. She said, "Your blood sugar might be low," and I accepted a slice of cheese and a glass of orange juice. I called Phil, who was home that day, from her kitchen phone, and he set up a doctor's appointment for that evening.

An electrocardiogram showed supraventricular tachycardia, a potentially dangerous heart rhythm. I consulted with a cardiologist who did a heart workup that included imaging. There was a hint of mitral valve prolapse. My rapid heart rate was deemed to be from anxiety; the arrhythmia was transitory. He prescribed the beta blocker, Corgard. My respirations and heart rate became more regular, and I felt calmer—for a while—but the horrible episodes of impending doom were still easily triggered. They had become a dreadful habit. Fear of passing out, going crazy, losing control, or imminent death continued to plague me. When an attack woke me, my heart raced so fast I couldn't feel it. I counted my pulse repeatedly during the day. I was obsessed. My husband encouraged me to get help.

I perused the local newspaper for a specialist in anxiety and panic and found a space ad for a psychiatrist. Dr. B. was middle-aged and relatable. He listened with apparent empathy to my stories of adoption, my father's authoritarianism, and my phobias.

Mary Ellen Gambutti

Wrecking Ball: A Darker Perspective

In the subway under Columbus Circle, Nana dropped our tokens into the slot of a wood and metal turnstile. It made a strange ratchet noise as she pushed us through. My hand in hers, we hurried into a subway car just as the engineer called out the next stop. The sliding doors hissed and snapped shut. Nana helped me climb onto the safety of a smooth wicker seat near a hot open-window breeze. The blur of cold white wall tile and black writing, the whir of ceiling fans, and the click-clack rhythm of the tracks as we picked up speed mesmerized me. The flash of overhead lights as we roared through the tunnels worried me, and I pressed against Nana's petite frame for protection.

We lurched to a stop with the screech and squeal of steel and were out in the piercing light and suffocating heat, the din and fumes of traffic. Horns blared, and the reek of overflowing trash barrels and dog piss stung my nose. Calls and shouts of workmen startled me. Red dust rose up from the empty lot across the street, where a lead wrecking ball swung like an enormous pendulum from a massive chain. The scene horrified me as I witnessed the relentless power to smash, crash, and crush a brick building. Overwhelmed and in tears, I couldn't hear Nana's voice, my source of consolation. She picked me up to cross MacDougal Street to the apartment building's stoop of her friend, Mrs. T.

This childhood memory encapsulated my trauma in a similar way to my panic at depth and height, the view from the Statue of Liberty when I was seven, and my terror of flying that formed during the flight from Tokyo at age twelve. Dr. B. wondered whether my mental turmoil—especially the night voices that made my psyche spin—might have stemmed from molestation by my father. I denied that possibility. It was during the time when women were coming forward with allegations about male relatives.

The doctor asked how I'd feel about taking a trial of lithium. He said I was possibly manic-depressive. I shied away from it but considered the chance that I was mildly bipolar. He prescribed benzodiazepines for generalized anxiety disorder (GAD).

I asked, "Does depression cause anxiety or the anxiety cause depression?"

"That's a good question," he said.

I'd long resigned myself to writing *adopted* on medical questionnaires. Dr. B. asked, "Have you given any thought to searching for your birth mother and birth records?"

"Maybe, but I don't know where to begin. All I have is my certificate of birth and baptism saying I was born in Rock Hill, South Carolina."

On his pad, he wrote his most effective remedy in the form of action. He gave me the name and number of a Philadelphia adoption support group, Adoption Forum, and with it, the impetus to search for my birth mother. I needed to find the truth of myself. I made the decision and would find I had the determination and persistence to search for my family of origin, although I knew less than nothing about them.

The light surfaced like a full moon through a stormy sky. A fog lifted. My eyelids peeled back, and I glimpsed an affirmation, a validation that I was unrelated to the family that raised me. It was not a myth. The shock of knowing I was relinquished hit me. My desperation had led to illumination—the severe panic attacks that brought me to the place to snip the veil of secrecy. I would find the truth of who I was. I had been aware in some way, from my early years, that adoption was what placed my parents and me together. Now, the gravity of what had occurred struck. All that it meant to be adopted. Now, I had to grieve for all I had lost and move forward to get what I could back.

$\sim$

Part Fourteen

Questa, a Fable

"The journey is the adoptee's heroic attempt to bring together the split parts of the self. It is an authentic way of being born again. It is a way of taking control of one's own destiny, of seizing power. It is a way of finding oneself."

—Betty Jean Lifton,
Journey of the Adopted Self

Adoption. It was a whisper. Questa worried when she was three or four that people might go away and not come back. Her father might not come back. Her grandparents might die. She wished hard to keep her granddaddy alive, because she could see he was the oldest.

Don't let them leave me. Don't let them go.

Her dad and mom told her a new story, out of the blue, about their love for her over all the others. A wondering came into her heart that she had never felt before. It was a dream about *missing ones,* people without names and faces. She couldn't conjure faces for the mother who didn't keep her, for the family that didn't stay.

Try as she might, Questa couldn't make herself remember *the lost ones*. There were no stories to help her see them. The more she longed, the more she believed in her ghost family. The more she was afraid. *One day I will know them, know who they are, my missing ones. I will dream them real.*

Her fear, pain, and questions came from the time before the memories had words.

What do I remember about another mother, my first mother? What did her voice sound like? What was the rhythm of her heartbeat? How did her skin feel to the touch? Did she smell good?

There were questions like *was I born from her belly? Where is she now?* She knew in her heart she couldn't ask her parents because they were the ones who saved her. Still, she grew up with that innate wish to find her mother. She would forever seek these answers and more. She would never stop thinking about her missing people. Questa longed for a place of the heart. An unknown place of origin. A place in a wish.

She would search for her origin when the time felt right, although she had no idea how she would search for the unknown woman. When Questa turned forty, her parents sent her papers they'd saved: court papers that assigned her, at a year old, to them but revealed little else. She turned to the southern state of her birth and baptism without a birth certificate. She turned to the agency that placed her with her mom and dad. She put all her energy and faith in the system but found it was a system that, after adoption, excluded her. She was able to learn that she was not born in the infant home but in St. Francis Hospital in Greenville, across the state. There was nothing more she could learn because the records were sealed. They would not confirm her family of origin.

Questa's two years of inquiries, persuasion, vague promises, and letters returned with regret left her with fading hope of finding her mother. She couldn't accept failure. When a crucial piece of information was revealed to her, she asked for help from a Greenville historian who delivered directories and old road maps that led Questa home.

Amid abundant warmth and welcome, Questa met her mother, the unmentioned woman with an unmentioned story but always wondered about. They were alike in hair and eye color, voice, and high cheekbones.

They had a year with each other to glean stories that had fallen into the gap of a lifetime. The name of Questa's father was still missing. Her mother's memory had faded from life's uncertainties, illness, need, and remorse—a life unexpressed except in the simplest of terms. In that year-long moment, the mother and Questa gave the best they could. Through the pain and confusion of loss, they enjoyed a loving acceptance—longing briefly rewarded, as on the day of Questa's birth.

Questa emerged from her greatest trial. She conquered her deepest longing and discovered new kinship. Restored, she embraced her unfathomable wish.

⁓

"The child separated from her mother at or soon after birth misses the mutual and deeply satisfying mother-child relationship, the roots of which lie in that deep area of personality where the physiological and psychological are merged."

—*Florence Clothier, 1943*

Courage to Act

My parents might have imagined I'd ask for more than my Certificate of Baptism and Birth someday but were waiting for me to broach the issue. All the while, I had been protecting them, shielding them from the potential hurt of my inquiries. How ironic that would have been! Maybe they kept the letters as mementos not meant to be shared with me. Mom did respond to my request for more documentation. In February 1992, she mailed me my original baptism and birth certificate, and I looked at it with mature eyes. She sent a pack of onionskin bound in a legal blue cover from a Rock Hill law firm, Spencer & Spencer.

I read with intense fascination the court transcript and signed adoption papers. Mom had enclosed a handwritten note: "I don't know why you would want these."

She was still in denial that it had meaning to me. With only myths, the truth of my identity gnawed at me until I resolved to cut through the secrecy. I became more determined with each new fragment and was soon driven by the momentum of my discoveries.

The adoption papers revealed a striking piece of information: I was a child petitioner! I had a guardian ad litem, Sister Mathias! Someone knew me as Ruth Ann! Handwritten and typed letters, still in their envelopes, between my parents and the adoption agency were included in Mom's manila envelope. With these contents, I focused on possible contacts and began to assemble a picture of the process of my adoption.

Elements of my search coincided. When I initiated calls and letters, my obsessive nature propelled the search. I was working and going to school part time for horticulture and made calls when I had time. It was the Dark Ages before computers and the internet. I had a portable electric type-writer, a landline phone, and an overactive mind.

While my search was beginning to surge, my husband and I planned an island trip and needed passports. Phil had his birth certificate, and I had my trusty certificate from St. Anne's parish in Rock Hill. I couldn't get a passport in Philadelphia with it; it wasn't a state-issued document. As a military dependent, there had been no problem getting a passport, but I was told by the authorities that I would need my original birth certificate.

I pictured my birth certificate in a vault, like a safe deposit box, with all my original family's identifying information: my infant story and my identity locked away at the South Carolina State Bureau of Vital Statistics.

On September 23, 1992, I sent eight dollars and a request for my original birth certificate to record retrieval at the South Carolina Department of Health and Environmental Control Division of Vital Records.

October 5, 1992, the Department of Health supervisor wrote, telling me of their requirement of an adoption decree in addition to other information I was not able to provide. She called to tell me she would contact Catholic Charities directly to get the identifying information she needed to search for my record. She may then be able to forward me an amended record.

I paid fifty dollars and, in a few weeks, received something called an amended birth certificate. No birth mother's name, just my adoptive parents' names typed on a white paper and the place of my birth, St. Francis Hospital in Greenville. My birth was verified at 1:00 a.m. by the attending physician, Dr. Geronimo. I discovered years later in a computer data scan that he was the common entry for

Catholic Charities and poverty cases in the Greenville area.

The white card, stamped with the South Carolina state seal, was an interesting artifact, but it didn't bring me peace of mind. Though I was on fire to keep learning, I could not have access to my original birth records. No imprinted baby feet. I wrote to St. Francis Hospital, and the records administrator said there was nothing. They had been destroyed, perhaps by the early version of the shredder—the incinerator.

As a teen, I'd been off-handed when asked "Do you want to know who your real parents are?" "No," I'd say in a brave, noble voice, "my parents are the only ones I have." I tried to convince myself I had no interest in anything related to my adoption or original family, because I thought it was forbidden territory. All of it was unknowable. It was too overwhelming to comprehend. My denial was born of my fear of losing the people closest to me.

Correspondence

Bolstered with my needed antianxiety medication and my newlyn won passport, we took our vacation in St. Lucia. When we returned, my husband accompanied me to a winter evening meeting in Philadelphia of Adoption Forum, the referral the psychiatrist had given me weeks ago. With their blessing, guidance, references, and instructions, I mapped a tentative course. I had to contact Catholic Charities to obtain my nonidentifying information. I might get minimal information from the adoption agency that placed me with Al and Agnes Caffrey in 1952.

My first letter seems tentative, self-effacing—almost apologetic.

February 15, 1992
The Director
Catholic Charities of Charleston
Dear Sir or Madam:

I am a forty-year-old woman who, in 1951, presumably at birth, was relinquished to St. Philip's Mercy Hospital, then in Rock Hill. I was placed about one year later in a loving home, within which I reached maturity. I must confess, however, to a void in my life and the need to know more about my identity and the possibility of living natural family members.

My adoptive parents have always made me aware that I was adopted. I am in possession, at my request, of the adoption papers, so I have a few of the puzzle pieces.

I would greatly appreciate any information you could provide me so I might share the knowledge of my origins and medical history with my twenty-year-old daughter. Specifically, I am seeking information about whether my parents handed me to Philip's Mercy Hospital themselves, whether I have siblings (alive or deceased), the surname and nationality of my birth family, my actual birthplace, my parents' ages at my birth, and any available medical history.

Thanking you in advance for any information you can send me or, in place of actual documentation, the name of the person or agency I should contact for this information so valuable to me.

Yours truly,
Mary Ellen C.

Facts in hand:

Date Adoption Filed, County of York
Name of child: Ruth Ann
DOB 9/21/51
Catholic Charities Representative: Rev. M. Shean, The
Oratory, Rock Hill, SC
St. Philip's Infant Home Representative and Super-
intendent of St. Philip's Mercy Hospital: Sr. Mathia
Attys: Spencer and Spencer, Rock Hill, SC

From Catholic Charities of Charleston:

Feb. 19, 1992

I shall be happy to tell you what I may. The only informa-
tion we may share with you is the non-identifying kind.
Your birth mother insisted she did not know who
the father was; consequently, we have no information
on him. She had been married but was divorced. There
was one child from this marriage, but the name is such
that it is impossible to tell whether the child was a boy
or girl. Because your birth mother and her child were
living with her parents when she became pregnant with
you, she believed it impossible to ask them to take the
responsibility of another child. Out of loving concern
for you and so that you might have the love and care
of two parents, she asked Catholic Charities to assume
custody and place you in an adoptive home.

Birth Mother
Age: 27

Religion: Baptist
Education: 4th grade (had to leave school to help at home)
Occupation: Textile Worker
Height: 5' 7" [my note—same as mine]
Weight: 165 lbs [same build as mine)
Color Eyes: Brown [same]
Color Hair: Brown [same]

Regarding the medical background, there were no known hereditary illnesses, and she had never had any serious illness.

I regret that there is so little I have to share with you, but perhaps a few of your questions have been answered.

Sincerely yours,
Sister Elaine Johnson
Adoption Worker

Although it wasn't nearly as much as I wanted, this tidbit of nonidentifying information did give me a profile of my birth mother. Our likenesses could be quite alike. My imagination was running wild. I was even more determined to find my lost mother, and I read anything I thought could give me direction.

In early August, I wrote to Adoptees & Birthparents in Search, a referral from Adoption Forum. In turn, Mary Bishop in Greenville, South Carolina, referred me to Karen Connor, director of Adoptees & Birthparents in Search in West Columbia. Dated 8/18/92, a yellow sticky note from Karen Connor on the forms she sent reads, "Please fill out registry form and return with $25. We can often help with searches such as yours."

Karen replied when she received the nonidentifying information and my twenty-five dollar registry-membership check.

Sept. 4, 1992
Dear Mary Ellen,

I am happy to report I feel I can be of some help to you. I can get the last name for you at birth and possibly your birth mother's name. The person I know who can get this information for you charges $50. If you will send me this amount, I'll see what I can do. I will warn you though, that Catholic Charities kept very poor records. I cannot guarantee the total accuracy of the information. By this, I mean the spelling is off a little or a piece of information is missing. But then $50 is not too much for someone who is sticking their neck out.

On my forty-second birthday, September 21, 1992, I wrote to Catholic Charities for more complete information after I learned from Karen Connor that Sister Elaine Johnson had retired.

Catholic Charities
1662 Ingram Road
Charleston, SC 29407
September 21, 1992
To the Director:

Your records will show that I have exchanged correspondence with Sister Elaine Johnson. Earlier this year, and she was kind enough to give me nonidentifying information regarding my birth mother.

My adoption into the Caffrey home was finalized in 1952. My date of birth is 9/21/51. Sister Elaine indicated that my birth mother had one child from a previous marriage, that it was impossible to tell the sex of the child due to the ambiguity of the name. I would greatly appreciate your telling me how old my brother or sister was at the time of my birth. Thank you for assisting me with information so vital to me.

Yours sincerely,
Mary Ellen Caffrey Gambutti

Marie Lescord of Catholic Charities called as soon as she received my letter. While she spoke, I penned notes with intense urgency in blue ink at the top and around the margins of my copy of the letter I'd mailed to the director of Catholic Charities. Her yet-non-identifying narrative gave me some solace and a little more information.

I followed up with Karen Connor.

October 9, 1992

Dear Karen. I have been in touch with Maria Lescord, who is Sister Elaine's replacement at Catholic Charities. She called to give me additional non-identifying information very graciously, indicating she liked to "stretch" the amount of information she could legally give adoptees. And so, this is about it. I hope this helps me find out who my family is.

My birth mother's birthday is 2/16/24. She was 23 when she first married. She was married for one year when she separated from her husband and was pregnant with her first child at the time. She went to

live with her parents, and her child was born 8/15/48,
making him or her almost three years old at the time
of my birth 9/21/51. The child's name appears twice
in the document as "Karn." Obviously, this could be
a misspelled Karen but maybe not.

Maria also told me my birth mother's parents
had been farmers all their lives in the Greenville area
and that my birth mother left school in fourth grade
to help on the farm. At the time of my birth, she was
employed as a textile worker. There were two brothers
and one sister to my birth mother. All of them were
living in the Greenville area. Reverend James Sharples
was the director of Catholic Charities at the time of
my birth, and he stated that my mother insisted she
did not know who my father was.

I requested a copy of my birth certificate from
Mrs. Jo Ann Gooding, supervisor of certification at the
Office of Vital Records and Public Health Statistics in
Columbia, and she indicated that there is no record
filed under my adoptive family name and that I need
to give her the certified order for adoption. She asked
for the name of the hospital I was born in., but I'm only
guessing if I say it was St. Philip's Mercy. So once she
found out I was adopted through Catholic Charities,
it seems she'll call them and get the information she
needs. Seems unfair she can get it and I can't search
for my file. So we'll see what comes of this. Assuming
she sends me an "amended document," as she said she
then would, will this be of any use to us? I hope so!

Best wishes,
Mary Ellen Gambutti

I accomplished little in my search through the rest of 1992, after I sent Karen fifty dollars for someone to "stick her neck out" and find my name at birth, and hopefully, give me my birth mother's name.

Karen's reply came the following April.

April 14, 1993
Adoptees & Birth Parents in Search
Dear Mary Ellen,

I apologize for taking so long to write back. I have really been hoping to have more information for you by now, as my "contact" said they would try to obtain more. Now I feel they will be unable to get us further information, and I'm afraid we have only this much to work with. All they could get is that at the time of your birth, your name was Ruth Ann Lee. You were born at the St. Francis Hospital in Greenville, South Carolina. There was a date of 3/52 on something, but they could not decipher what it applied to.

This is all that I can provide at this time. Perhaps if you write to Greenville Public Library, they can send you photocopies of the LEE listings in the Green-ville City Directory for the years 1950 and 1951, etc.

I sure wish that I could be a further help...Please keep in touch and let me know what you find out.

Sincerely,
Karen Connor, Director

My name at birth was Ruth Ann Lee! It wasn't a guarantee that my birth mother's name was Lee or that Lee was my biological father's name. Karen Connor had "really been hoping to have more information" for me between September and April.

I contacted the Greenville Public Library, as Karen suggested, and they put me in touch with Anne McKuen, a local historian and researcher. I requested that she send me photocopies of the Lee listings in the Greenville City Directory for 1950 and 1951, as Karen Connor suggested. Anne charged a modest hourly rate to do the research. I allowed myself renewed hope. Using the Lee listing from Anne, I made a few potshot calls into the Greenville area.

June 2, 1993
Karen Connor
Director, Adoptees & Birth Parents in Search
Post Office Box 5551
West Columbia, South Carolina 29171
Dear Karen,

It was good to talk with you the other day. Maybe I should update my reunion registry. Since the time I joined ABI, some things have changed. Can you send me a form, please?

I cannot get marriage records from the DHS (Department of Human Services) other than a statement of marriage for Karn Lee, since I am told only parents or children can get the records for marriage licenses and applications. What they'll give me is basically what I give them back in statement form: bride's full name, date of birth, and marriage date and place. I can't believe how difficult it is to get information from Vital Statistics! I do feel stymied.

Prompted by questions from Anne McKuen, I contacted Marie Lescord at Catholic Charities again, not telling her I know my last name. I asked her if it is possible to tell me:

1. *The county and or township where my birth mother's farm was*
2. *Whether my sibling, "Karn" had the same surname as my birth mother's family*
3. *Whether my mother's siblings (two males, one female) worked in mills or were farmers and what township they lived in*
4. *Whether I lived with my family for a while before I was relinquished and for how long (I was taken home by my adoptive family on February 28, 1952, from St. Philip's Mercy in Rock Hill)*
5. *The location or township of the mill where my mother worked*
6. *My grandfather's first initial*

We'll see. I wonder if you can tell me in South Carolina who can get sealed records opened and which court can unseal them. What facts and circumstances meet South Carolina requirements to open sealed records? Any chance of finding a sympathetic judge who will read a heartfelt letter and possibly a letter from a physician? Would this go to Rock Hill, where I was adopted? Please comment on these questions if you have a chance. Also if you do think of any other leads, please let me know. Thanks ever so much.

Sincerely,
Mary Ellen Gambutti

Among the resources in the red Adoption Forum folder was the book *Lost and Found* by Betty Jean Lifton, and I immediately purchased it. Her words spoke directly to my heart. From her I learned of Jean Paton, an adoptee and advocate for adoptee voices. E. Wayne Carp, her biographer, wrote about the activist's fifty-year struggle to reform American adoption. I share his description of his book *Jean Paton and the Struggle to Reform American Adoption* with his permission. Excerpted from "About Jean Paton and This Book" at *The Biography of Jean Paton* website at https://jeanpaton.com/about-e-wayne-carp/.

...Paton, a twice-adopted, ex-social worker, founded the Life History Study Center (1953) and Orphan Voyage (1962) the research and communications center for adopted adults. She gave adult adoptees a voice and provided them with a healthy self-image; facilitated thousands of meetings between adult adoptees and their families of origin; fought tirelessly to open sealed adoption records, and indefatigably explained the adoption experience to a wider public. Paton's ceaseless activity created the preconditions for the explosive emergence of the adoption reform movement in the 1970s. She played a prominent role in the formation of the first national organization for birth parents, Concerned United Birthparents, and was instrumental in the creation of the first national organization for adult adoptees, the American Adoption Congress. By the 1970s, Paton emerged as an influential presence on the national and international stage, inspiring adoption reformers spanning the English-speaking world. Paton received awards and

tributes, but none pleased her more than the sobriquet bestowed on her, as early as 1981, as the "Mother of the adoption reform movement." Paton's struggle to reform American adoption was never easy; she faced resistance at every turn. This, then, is Jean Paton's story: one courageous woman's struggle to overcome American society's prejudice against adult adoptees and women who gave birth out of wedlock; reverse social workers' harmful policy and practice concerning adoption and sealed adoption records, and change lawmakers enactment of laws prejudicial to adult adoptees and birth mothers."

I wrote:

June 10, 1993
Jean Paton
Orphan Voyage
2141 Road 230 Cedaredge, Colorado 81413
Dear Ms. Paton:

I am writing this after reading Jean Lifton's book Lost and Found. *I have been trying to get records together for a little over a year now, and I'm at the point where I feel stymied. I will tell you a bit of my story, and perhaps you would be able to offer some insight as to a logical next step.*

I was born Ruth Ann Lee at St. Francis Hospital Greenville, South Carolina (they have destroyed those medical records). I have my amended birth certificate. I do not know my mother's name, but she was born in 1924. I'm working under the assumption that her

*maiden name is Lee, since she was married for a
year, three years before my birth, then divorced, and
returned home with her infant. I can get no further
information for Vital Statistics. I am only working
on hunches for the family's area. Can you advise
of any concrete move I can make to wrangle some
additional information? Catholic Charities won't
go any further. I have worked with Karen Connor
of Adoptees & Birthparents in Search in Columbia,
SC, and she suggested calling from a phone directory
of "Lee's" in the targeted area. I wonder if there is an
alternative. I would be very grateful if you could give
me some direction.*

Very truly yours,
Mary Ellen Gambutti

Her return note, and the information she sent with it, provided a breath of air along my tiring journey.

From the desk of Orphan Voyage 6/19/93

*Dear Mary Ellen, There are some very good genealo-
gists in your area of PA. There was one Walter Sheppard, who understood our plight very well. Maybe
he is still around. That's all I can come up with in
addition to what you have done.*

Sincerely,
Jean Paton

At Jean Paton's suggestion, I wrote to Philadelphia genealogist Walter Sheppard. He, in turn, directed me to a South

Carolina genealogist and historian, Gelee Corley Hendricks. She sent me a wealth of information and guidance.

In the meantime, a woman called—was she from Catholic Charities?—odd for me not to write down her name—after my follow-up note to Marie Lescord. I had asked Marie six specific questions, reiterated to Karen Connor in my letter of June 2.

The woman said she might be able to give me more if I would send her fifty dollars and would call me back when she received the payment. Whether cash or check, or to whose attention, I can't recall. She called back as she said she would and told me my mother's name: Leila Grace Cox.

I was stunned—it did feel like I was in a dream—amazed that this angel had risked her job to help an adult adoptee find her truth. Marie had said that she liked to "stretch" non-identifying information, and it seems possible that she was the caller. What would have transpired to effect this release of my birth mother's name? Had there been communication between Karen Connor and Catholic Charities? I would bet on it, and I am still deeply grateful.

I now had something big to give to Gelee Corley Hendricks: my mother's family name, Cox. Gelee wrote back to me on letterhead with the official Genealogical Society seal. She reported that she had called a genealogy colleague and Greenville native, a woman named Catherine Hester, who had done cemetery surveys and typed the five volumes that were donated and published by the Greenville chapter of the South Carolina Genealogical Society.

Catherine, who was retired, had "contributed cursory information that could be very useful to you if documented," Gelee said. "The Greenville County census could yield the family units, and death certificates that begin in 1915 are supposed to give birth parents if known. These are available up to 1941 at the SC archives in Columbia." Gelee sent me volume two of the cemetery survey. It was for Antioch Christian Cemetery, the burial place of many Cox family members.

Catherine was familiar with my mother's ancestral family name, Cox, but what was most helpful was she knew the burial location of a prominent head of the family. John Quincy Cox was born 10 October 1856 and died 24 November 1924, and his wife Mary Henriette Lenderman was born 1 November 1858 and died 5 November 1928. Gelee (per Catherine's phone call) listed their child as Frank A. Cox, who married Corrie Henderson. Frank and his wife had a daughter named Leila Grace Cox, born 16 February 1924.

Gelee also sent me photocopies of a few old local maps, designating Antioch and the homesteads of Cox and Lenderman as well as homes of other Antioch church families whose graves were listed in the survey. I got in touch with Anne McKuen again to request new directories, this time for Cox, and she sent me listings and obituaries. My search took off!

It had been a team effort, but it was the breakthrough of identifying information that did it. Gelee, Catherine, and Anne pinpointed the location of my ancestral farms, and my drive put me in that place.

The crucial piece had been the revelation from an angel at Catholic Charities that Cox was my mother's maiden name, not Lee. I wrote to Marie Lescord again, but there was no reply, and I moved on from Catholic Charities for a time.

When I held copied drawings and images, news clippings, and obituaries with dates before the Civil War, my spirit soared, not with panic but with a longing that stirred my heart of hearts. In the process of discovering immediate connections, I experienced the pull of my ancestral family and the urgency to learn about and lay my eyes on all, greedy to make contact with all who might remain from my family of origin. The result of the cascade of calls and letters that had occupied my free time for over a year was the critical puzzle piece: my birth mother's maiden name, Leila Grace Cox.

Mirrors of Loss: A Haibun

I can talk about how my mother surrendered me. Although a newborn, I knew. It mattered. That she held me for nine months and might not have remembered, and in her arms for a brief hello, I remember.

At six, I learned my parents were not the ones. A deep flood of fear and questions arose. Would there, could there be another separation, any other separation? I feared what new separation could—no—would bring.

Worry haunted me into my twenties and thirties. Inevitable, cruel separation, fear of final separation. There would be, and it would be my doing, my fault. The panic of ultimate loss—loss of self.

I formed identity through loss without a living person to look in the eye or in the mirror to recognize until this daughter bore a daughter, until after a long search I found my elderly birth mother and my birthright of living kin.

Kin. The wow of reunite, recovery, realization. My fear abated in the knowing. Maybe her fears did too. Lessened, never lost.

Mary Ellen Gambutti

a sheer scrim ripples
over a girl's image
waking to now

(Haibun is a Japanese poetic form that combines Haiku verse and prose.)

Part Fifteen

Assembling the Pieces

"Who in the world am I? Ah, that's the great puzzle."

—Lewis Carroll,
Alice's Adventures in Wonderland

1. Wash Day

Nana was in charge of the laundry room, the unfinished side of the basement where her Maytag wringer washer was, for many years, stationed in front of two smooth, built-in concrete washtubs. "I won't use that thing," she said quietly of the new washing machine. She used the reliable Maytag, the one she'd owned since 1928, where it sat on the front porch of the Pennsylvania clapboard house she and Mike rented from the mining company. It ran by diesel. When Granddaddy trucked it to their most recent New York apartment, he wired an electric motor to it. It still needed to be lubricated, and Nana kept a flat enamel pan under it to catch oil drips.

From the time I was four, the rhythm and hum of the motor, the soft clunk of the agitator, and the swish of suds interested me. "Here, make yourself useful," Nana said, handing me a little muslin bag tied with white string, "to whiten the clothes." I'd let it drop into the rinse tub on the left side and watch blue swirl against the cold water. She cautioned and showed me how to feed Granddaddy's wet socks through the wringer and how to retrieve them on the other side. I released them to swim in the blue rinse.

Nana and I sang as we worked. While she washed Granddaddy's greasy work clothes, she sang in a plaintive voice, one of the hard-luck songs from the Great Depression, the story of the drunken spouse and orphaned daughter, a sad song she taught my mother.

> *Mother, oh why did you leave me alone,*
> *No one to comfort, no friends, and no home?*
> *Dark is the night when the storm rages wild*
> *God pity Bessie, the drunkard's lone child...*

Nana flipped off the motor switch and pulled the cord to the ceiling light bulb. She hoisted the bushel basket of wet clothes onto her left hip, and we climbed the concrete cellar steps. I remember her steady, determined footfalls on the steps to the roof of her Fifty-Eighth Street apartment. We crossed the grass in the sunshine to the metal pole that opened up and could twirl like an umbrella. I picked out clothespins from the hanger bag and held them up two at a time. Some were spring hinged, and some reminded me of gingerbread men. She held one between her lips while pinning a shirttail to the line and then took it out to pin up the other tail. I imitated her. I liked the woodiness of the clothespins and their taste between my lips. Nana bent for a blouse, towel, or Granddaddy's trousers, and then reached to fasten them to the revolving plastic lines, her motions a rhythm. Her housedress rippled in the sweet summer breeze, a world away from the Pennsylvania farm where she hung up her uncle's farm clothes and later her husband's coal-dirty overalls.

2. A Borrowed Homestead

In 1971, among my favorite music were Grateful Dead; Joni Mitchell; Crosby, Stills, Nash, and Young; The Byrds; Bob Dylan; Joan Baez; and John Sebastian. Both sexes wore long hair and jeans; sandals, hiking boots, or fringed moccasins. In flowy shirts and granny dresses, girls were often braless. I was tall and fresh faced, and aspired to a romanticized version of American life as it had been 125 years earlier.

Tom and I were newlyweds when we stepped out of a middle-class New Jersey town into an idyll of self-sufficiency—as we perceived it—in the gilded countryside of the Susquehanna River Valley, where we lived, for a time, with Sally and Jeff. The 1920s farmhouse rental was sixty-five dollars a month, the electric power was off by the tenants' choice, and the house had never been plumbed, so there was no running water, and no hand pump in the kitchen sink that Jeff salvaged and piped out to the porch. We drank, cooked, washed dishes, and bathed in fresh water we bailed and hauled in galvanized buckets, sloshing up the slope from the creek by the house from the clear, icy spring. We lit kerosene lamps, heated with a potbellied stove, and baked, sautéed, and boiled on the old kitchen woodstove left by the landlord.

We thought we were living free on our planet, like the *Whole Earth Catalog* and artists like Alicia Bay Laurel taught. I felt the hope of nature, dreaming like a child might of open fields, trees, and gardens.

Jeff had a passion for foraging wild plants, and we studied the book by the rugged edible plant stalker, Euell Gibbons, *Stalking the Wild Asparagus, Field Guide Edition*. In damp April, we collected morels in a derelict peach orchard and gently placed the wizened, musky, wrinkled mushrooms in a willow basket. At home, Sally threaded them to hang over the kitchen wood stove to dry with last year's red peppers. We sautéed them with field onions and folded them into omelets. Jeff showed us how to harvest fragrant roots of sarsaparilla and steep them into a noncarbonated, root beer-tasting ale.

Blue mason jars packed with peaches, cherries, squash, and beans lined the dusty, old shelves along the funky cellar stairs. Sliced apples, spread on racks in the upstairs south-facing bedroom and dried, were as sweet as candy. We picked snow peas and plump tomatoes in bare feet and baggy, faded Levi's purchased at an Amish tag sale in town.

We plucked spicy violet leaves and winter cress from the field, and they merged with cultivated greens, peas, and tomatoes in the wooden salad bowl. In good weather, we enjoyed meals and shared stories on the rustic back porch. At breakfast, we cozied up to fresh brown eggs Brian had collected, buckwheat pancakes slathered with wild elderberry compote, and Sally's dense brown bread, smeared with local honey. After a supper of salad, rice and beans, or soup, we lingered on the porch or in the parlor, read, and chatted until the children slept and our eyes grew tired in the dim light.

Sally rose early to bake pies and bread in the woodstove, and the aroma of fruit, yeast, and the browning crust woke us. The old Hoosier cabinet stored the dishes and provided counter and workspace. Walnut Acres, the natural foods grocery at Penn's Creek, sold grains and flours bagged in bulk, and peanut butter in big metal bins.

In the winter, the parlor stove pipe rising through the ceiling adequately heated two of the three upstairs bedrooms. Sally and Jeff moved from the bedroom they used in summer on the north side to one of the southern-exposed rooms, and the children slept in their little wooden rope beds in the room next to their parents. Tom and Jeff brought down the extra bed to the parlor for Tom and me, cozy by the Franklin stove, as it might have been in by-gone days during winters' worst.

Eighty-eight year old Elmer, the landlord, was charming and weathered like the old farmhouse. He liked to visit his tenants occasionally, especially Sally, and would steer an ancient tractor across his fallow pasture from another house he owned and had moved to years ago when his wife died. Sally's tousled blonde hair, her plain housedress, her soap and water homespun looks, might have reminded him of her, and the joys and hardships of the life they'd had there, farming and raising a family. When she caught sight of him driving toward the house, Sally hurriedly swept crumbs into a kitchen corner, standing the broom to hide them.

The summer sunlight shone down the lane as I squinted a glance across the garden. Nana was striding past the barn in a home-sewn pink cotton shirtwaist dress and slip-on sneakers. *Can I believe my eyes? They must be fooling me!* I blinked, and there she was, her bright smile and open wave as she walked toward me. "Nana! What a surprise!"

There was no phone, so Nana stopped by unannounced, having driven alone from the family home in New Jersey. Route 80 had recently been completed, and she knew her way around the rural roads she had traveled since her youth. Nana was visiting Granddaddy's sister, Mable, and her husband, Elmer. When I was five, I visited their dairy farm with Nana and Granddaddy. Mable poured me a glass of fresh milk from a big tin can with a handle. She pumped cold, sweet water into a glass for me at the kitchen sink.

I had written to Mom and Nana that I was newly pregnant, and to let them know where we were, but I never expected to see her there. As it is so often with young people, I hadn't gotten in touch with Mable, but she directed Nana to the country road and the mailbox with the sunshine painted on it.

I hugged Nana and welcomed her to the porch and into the parlor of this primitive Middleburg farmhouse. She sat on the shabby, maroon velvet sofa, and I joined her with glasses of cooled mint tea. She could have been royalty.

On my eighteenth birthday, Nana had given me much more than a new oil lamp, washboard, wood hand-crank ice cream maker, and her handmade quilt. Those gifts signified what I would continue to cherish: the old-fashioned objects that represent humanity, hard work, and humility. But I didn't have to tell my nana that our rustic experiment, however liberating at the moment, had failed in the dust. She knew all along it would.

Jeff and Tom built a tepee with slender winter-toppled saplings they gathered from roadside woodlands. This summerhouse stood on the high field not far from the house.

Tom and I brought our baby girl, born in New Jersey, to visit our friends at the farmstead. We sheltered in the tepee one or two nights. Wild strawberries were plentiful in that south-facing field above the creek bank. The baby-sized fruits ripened quickly on the green, exposed hill, the tiny vines twisting and spreading their delicate white rosettes. One June day, our baby sat with her back against the blue sky and held a tiny strawberry between her thumb and forefinger, sampling its bitter sweetness. I was crossed-legged in faded jeans, and Tom lounged in the sunshine. Such a moment of pure innocence might have lasted a lifetime.

3. Grove Farmstead

When I imagine my natural great-grandmother, Mary Henriette, she piles and twists her long, dark hair up high, ties a muslin apron behind her back, and pins its bib to the bodice of her ankle-length calico work dress. She is brown eyed, strong, and tall, born in 1868 on a Greenville autumn day ninety-three years before my birth.

Mary Lenderman leaves her father's home at twenty-six to marry a neighbor, John Cox, who farms seventy acres of rich loam in a place called Grove, near the Fork Shoals of the Reedy River. In those post-Civil War days, as the second surviving daughter of a prominent Greenville farmer and soldier, Mary takes on the housekeeping and care of the little ones when her mother dies. Together, John and Mary have eleven children while she continues to care for a few of her youngest siblings. Among the brood is Frank Cox, my birth mother's father.

Before sunlight stirs the little ones, Mary stokes the wood-burning range while John completes the morning chores with the boys. Children's voices fill Mary's day. Eva, Lizzie, and Leila help roll out dough for loaves and biscuits from wheat and corn ground in the Lenderman's mill.

Her summer kitchen is alive with the garden's harvest.

Glass jars filled with summer green beans, okra, corn kernels, peaches, plums, sweet corn, sweet peppers, tomatoes, jellies, and jams sparkle on her pantry shelves.

On wash day, the boys build a wood fire a distance from the house and then haul water from the well to spill into two large tubs. One is set on the coals to boil; the other is for the rinse. Mary makes cake soap from lard and lye, and with her strong hands and arms, she scrubs the clothes on her wood and rippled glass washboard. She agitates the soapy water with a wooden posser. Until she can modernize with soap powder and a wooden washing machine equipped with a mangle, she twists the heavy, wet clothes in her strong hands and plunges them into the tub of cold water. She twists them again and hangs them between two wooden poles to dry.

4. Leila, Lost and Found

"...The questions arose in the children in the little houses: Was I born, where are those first people. What are they like? Could we meet someday? The questions were also in the minds of parents who were living in the wilderness: Where is my child? Is he all right? Does he know about me? Is he angry with me? Such simple and questioning people we are!"

—From Jean Paton's note mailed to those who inquire for help with their searches.

Phil and I sold our townhouse and were about to leave the suburbs for a Bucks County mini farm we purchased in the late summer of 1994. The movers had taken most of the furniture from the townhouse. I sat cross-legged in jeans on the blue bedroom carpet, focused on calling Greenville Coxes. Ready with a white, push-button landline phone, the manila envelope with Anne McKuen's Xerox copies of phone listings and maps, a yellow-lined pad, and a Bic pen.

I punched in the number for Lawrence M. Cox. "I'm looking for Leila Cox, daughter of Frank. Can you point me in the right direction?"

Without hesitation, a man replied, "I might be able to locate her. I'm the son of Lawrence Cox, one of Frank Cox's brothers."

His slow, easy drawl was corn on the cob and fried chicken. My heart thumped under my T-shirt. He responded to my non-Southern tone, my direct honesty.

"I believe I'm her daughter. I was adopted in 1952."

He continued, "I think Leila now lives with Karen."

It was the start of a loving friendship with my cousin, Lawrence, his wife, Doris, and his sister, Helen. As Lawrence spoke, I sketched the links and lines of his siblings' families, aunts, and uncles. Mary Henriette Lenderman and John Quincy Cox were his grandparents, my great-grandparents.

Just after five the same evening, I called Karen, my half-sister, and met her hurried hello. My air of confidence masked a heart that fluttered like a sparrow's. "May I speak with Leila, please?"

She replied, "I'm her daughter. What's this about?"

"I believe I'm her daughter too!"

There, I said it!

Karen's terse reply took me aback. "I always wondered if there were others!"

Nonetheless, relief flooded and overtook my nervous adrenalin. *Were there others besides us?* Our urgent voices gripped the moment. *Who are you? Who are we? Tell me all you can!*

I gushed like a fountain, "I've been searching for over a year and finally had the right clues for where to find kin! I'm so thrilled to talk to you!"

The tone of Karen's response changed to one of familiarity. "Leila put up with thirty-seven years of misery with a man in Texas. They moved from rental to rental in San Antonio. Their daughter, Susan, drowned in the creek at a large gathering in 1974. She was an epileptic, sixteen years old."

"Momma's had a bad year. She's been on insulin for eighteen years, and she's a bad housekeeper. In April 1992, she stepped on an insulin syringe needle. Her infection went to gangrene, and her leg had to be amputated little by little. My boyfriend urged me to go down to see her when the hospital called. I hadn't seen her for five years. She went into a convalescent home for four months, then a nursing home. In the meantime, her husband, Frank, died in a nursing home in July."

"When the doctor cleared her for travel, Dennis and I drove down again, cleaned out her place, and brought her home. Last week, I moved her into a seniors' apartment in Spartanburg because she couldn't cope with my two sons in a two-bedroom trailer. Momma's not used to kids."

My urgency had been clairvoyant. My birth mother had called to my heart—coming home to Greenville. It was time to make contact. Karen felt our mother should be told. After she broke the news to Momma the next day, Karen called me. I was as excited as she sounded to me. The truth of our relationship was established. About my call to her the day before, she said, "I was coming in with groceries when you called, and with your Northern accent, I thought you might be a bill collector wanting Momma, but as you kept on, I plopped the bags on the counter and slid down the wall with the phone. So glad! I suspected for years there were others. Aunt Ruth thought Momma might have had a boy and a girl, maybe twins."

As my call with Karen continued, she prefaced the dialog she'd had earlier with our mother with, "Her mind is sharp but sometimes hazy, due to her past." Leila had confessed reluctantly through her vague, troubled memory.

"Momma, a lady called from up North. She thinks she's your daughter."

"Not true!"

"Now, Momma, why would this lady call if she wasn't looking for you?"

"Yes, it's true. I just couldn't tell you. I had a baby girl when you were two. I just couldn't tell you. I passed out on the steps of St. Francis Hospital. After she was born, I got up and left, didn't bring her home. I thought the nuns would take good care of her."

Karen later told me that our mother's parents, who Karen lived with in her early years, may have realized their daughter was pregnant, but they never let on.

Happiness coursed through the phone lines and my veins when I spoke with my birth mother for the first time later that day, my anticipation eased by her soft, plain voice.

"Hello. Is this Leila?"

"Yes, this is me."

"I was born in St. Francis Hospital on September 21, 1951. I think you are my mother. My given name is Ruth Ann."

"I believe so."

"I'm so happy to talk to you! How do you feel about my finding you?"

"I think it's just great! So pleased!" Her voice was soft and sure.

I ventured further. "They make it very hard to connect. I don't think that's right."

"No, not if you *really* want to know," said my birth mother.

My thoughts tumbled like butterflies around a sweetly blooming shrub. Leila's words were a salve that held promise to heal my heart. I didn't need to ask her about her heartbreak or whether she'd thought of me or mourned my loss.

She spoke tenderly. "I always wondered if you were okay. What kind of life you had."

"I had a good childhood. I was adopted by a military couple," I said, sparing her from what she wouldn't have wanted to hear.

I was well-prepared by the adoption advocacy group but couldn't have expected a better outcome. I heard about the denial by birth mothers, the refusal to connect with relinquished sons and daughters, and the devastation that results from a failed search.

Filled with self-doubt and hampered by my fear of flying, but with the help of Xanax from Dr. B., I departed on that October morning flight between the Lehigh Valley and Greenville-Spartanburg airports. I gazed out my window at a new chapter. I'd soon be reunited with Leila, the mother who gave me life. My pulse quickened as the escalator glided down to the baggage carousel, where I spotted my welcoming party. A woman beamed and waved. Karen, my half-sister, called my name in the drawl I recognized from our phone calls since my search bore fruit.

I stepped off the escalator, grinning. When I spoke with Leila by phone, she seemed excited, and Karen had assured me her Momma wanted the reunion. The "lost ones" I'd conjured since childhood resembled me more closely than my welcoming group, and a sense of unreality overtook me. Karen hugged me enthusiastically and quickly introduced me to Barbara, her slender daughter, and her sons, Josh—a tall, burley middle schooler—and Daniel, his affable elder brother. Karen looped her left arm under Leila's right elbow for support. "This is Momma, Leila Grace."

Leila had insisted on standing from her wheelchair and leaning onto her walker. The smile on the large woman who was my mother was warm. Perhaps I'd felt her tentative touch before the nurse swaddled me and took me away. I saw emotion fill her moist, puffy eyes. Was it a recollection? A sense of regret? Pride for her grown daughter? Was it the anxiety I knew so well? The relinquishment papers would have stated—and Catholic Charities affirmed when I sought information—the mothers were told they wouldn't see their babies again. Leila had dared not hope that the infant she'd left behind would return to her one day. I took charge of the feelings and wrapped my arms around her. "Hello, Momma! Great to see you!"

She yielded to my warmth and murmured something meant for the gods.

Leila's natural affection couldn't replace my adoptive mother's nurturing. Perhaps Agnes had intuited that she could not replace my biological mother. Her pain and mine—as I grew into a person *I* didn't know and *she* couldn't relate to or help—were tragic.

Karen prepared a simple meal for us all. I chatted with Leila as she rested in the recliner, her left leg prosthesis showing below her blue pastel pants. The cruel, red streak of her dialysis shunt scar was visible below the right sleeve of her floral cotton blouse. Her salt-and-pepper hair was cut short for the occasion. Her high chitter was like a gentle bird. All seven—Momma, Barbara, Josh, Daniel, Karen, her friend, Dennis, and I—squeezed together at the kitchen table, tucking into fried chicken, biscuits, gravy, green beans, sweet tea, and store-bought apple pie. Our feast was a modest celebration of family love.

After dinner, we perused photo albums and found a few pictures of Leila in her twenties and thirties, aunts and uncles I'd never know, and Karen's children as they grew up. None of my father. Maybe Leila recognized him in me, or maybe there would be a secret photo stashed away.

5. Karen

During my first of many trips to the Greenville area where we all were born, we became close friends, and Karen and I talked for hours at a time when we were alone. She remembered Grandma as a gentle, kind woman, but Grandpa's personality was different. He was considered the black sheep of the family. Frank Cox's parents, Mary Henriette Lenderman and John Quincy Cox, were prominent, well-to-do landowners and farmers. As accounted by his nephew, Lawrence, Frank attended seminary but didn't persevere. He was a sharecropper, casual laborer, and floor sweeper at Conestee Cotton Mill. To his credit, he did stay with Grandma Corrie to the end.

Karen later wrote me in one of many letters we exchanged over the years.

*Momma had a troubled relationship with her par-
ents. She was a confused teenager who felt like an
outsider. She left home at sixteen looking for love,
worked in bars, waitressing. War time, there were
military everywhere in Greenville. She married a
much older man and divorced him as soon as he left
for military service.*

*Daddy was stationed in Keesler AFB, and
Momma was working in a bar. When they discovered they were both from upstate South Carolina,
they decided to get married. She was 21 and he was
19, and they got married on October 1, 1947. They
rented an apartment in an old two-story house. It
wasn't but a month or so before she was pregnant
with me.*

*But Daddy was a young farm boy away from home
and didn't want to be married anymore. Momma
soon found out he was messing around with another
woman. Momma tried to harm herself—and me—by
putting her head in their gas oven. He and a neighbor
had to knock the door down to get in. She left him,
came back to Greenville, and filed for divorce. She said
she took her last army wife check to buy baby clothes
for me. I was born on August 15, 1948, at Greenville
General Hospital at 8:30 a.m. It was a Sunday morning, I weighed 8 pounds 13 ounces. She brought me to
live at her parents' home at Roper Mountain.*

*She probably stayed with them a while, but she
later came and went. When I was one, I fell through a
window and cut my arm. Grandma sent someone into
Greenville to get her where, I think, she was working
at a restaurant. I survived without stitches.*

I have a memory of going to Uncle Wilton's funeral in Columbia. It was raining hard, and Uncle Charlie carried me up a muddy road to the gravesite. That was in 1951, so Momma was expecting you, Mary Ellen.

I remember being three or four, and Momma came home for Christmas. She crawled into bed with Grandma and me. She was so cold. She had a doll and a white doll carriage for me. While Momma was still at Roper Mountain, Annie would come and stay too. I loved her, but there was always friction between her and Momma.

I started school at seven in 1955 at Laurel Creek. My first teacher was Mrs. Cook. On the first day of school, Grandpa got on the bus with me. I was very embarrassed. Before the year was out, Uncle Charlie took me and enrolled me at Fountain Inn Elementary. I loved living with his family. It was clean and nice, and I had pretty dresses to wear—Cousin Linda's hand-me-downs.

I was a little afraid of Uncle Charlie because he was gruff. I know now he was my best supporter. After that school term, Grandpa wanted me back, and Uncle Charlie wanted to adopt me. He took me to Charleston to talk with Momma, but she said no. I think he got frustrated and took me back to Grandpa. I was homesick and cried.

Grandpa sold the old place on Roper Mt., and we moved to Greenville and lived in a duplex mill house in Conestee with Aunt Annie and her husband, Luther Pace. They put me in Welcome Elementary. I can't remember the teacher's name—only there a short time. I had the measles as they were packing to move again.

They bought a house on Old 10-Yard Road near Traveler's Rest. I started second grade at Reed Elementary. My teacher was Mrs. Bishop, and she was so nice. I think I skipped third grade. I may have spent two years in second grade—the grandparents never pushed school. If I didn't want to go, I just didn't.

My fourth-grade teacher was Mrs. Christine Kelso, and she gave me the love of reading. After lunch each day, she would make us rest while she read the Little House books to us. I still love them and have the whole series.

The summer I turned 11, Momma took me to Texas. The grandparents did not want me to go. We went to San Antonio, where she and her husband, Lee Adams lived, and by the time school started, we had moved to Abilene, Texas. I started fifth grade at Locust Street Elementary. My teacher was Mr. Austin. He was retired from the military, but he was a great teacher.

We lived at 1402 Cherry Street in a 1940s trailer. A woman named Mrs. Frederickson owned about six ancient trailers with a bathhouse—none had bathrooms—and one little one-room building that she rented out. I walked three to five blocks to school and came home for lunch. Momma would make me tomato soup and grilled cheese sandwiches.

We moved to Beeville, Texas, the next summer, and I started sixth grade at a newly built school, FMC Elementary, can't remember my teacher's name. I went there through Halloween. I remember trick or treating there. Back to San Antonio, we moved. Momma took me to a high school—I think she wasn't sure what grades the school had—and they tested me right then and said I was smart enough to be in seventh grade. I don't even remember the name of the school. I went there for a couple of weeks. I was so scared because I knew nothing about changing classes.

We moved back to Abilene, and I started seventh grade at Jefferson Junior High. We were back at that dumpy trailer park in a different trailer. My best friend was Linda Byrd. She lived across a small creek from us. She was in the eighth grade, and I thought she was so grown-up. I started eighth grade, same school. I was only there till October.

I don't remember Grandpa and Grandma doing Christmas at home, no tree or presents, but I remember being at Uncle Charlie's at Christmas. In my young eyes, it was beautiful and festive. Later, when I went to live with Momma, we didn't do Christmas either. On one Christmas, Frank gave me 1 dollar, and they waited in the car while I went into a dime store in Abilene. I bought a blank scrapbook. I kept it for years.

When I lived with Uncle Charlie and Aunt Ruth, at Easter, Linda and I had new dresses. Mine was mint green with a pleated skirt. Black patent leather shoes and a green ribbon tied in my hair over my new curly perm. Linda's was baby blue, and she wore a crinoline. I loved a skirt with a big crinoline under it. The Easter Bunny left us each a big basket of goodies on the front stoop. We each got two baby chicks—they were in shoeboxes. Mine were dyed green and the other fuchsia. I don't think they lived long.

One day we went to a small waterfall and pool
of water under it. Uncle Charlie picked me up and
threw me into the deep water. I cried and screamed
and thought I was drowning. Aunt Ruth told him,
"Charlie Cox, get her out, you're scaring her!" Of
course, he wouldn't have let me drown, but I didn't
know that. Maybe that is why I never learned to swim.
I still can't stand to have my head underwater.

Reading Karen's story, my narrative of a privileged adopted daughter panged and pierced me. I bemoan my many school transfers, but feel the sadness that stemmed from our mother's transience and instability, and its effect on my half-sister. When she was eight, she did move in with Charlie and Ruth. She needed the guidance she wasn't getting from her aging grandparents.

I'd learned from my nonidentifying information "the birth mother was in general good health at the time of her daughter's birth." Karen revealed that Stancel, Frank and Corrie's firstborn, died shortly after birth and was buried in Antioch, as are other infants. Leila's younger twin brothers, Milton and Wilton, were troubled. Wilton had severe epilepsy and accompanying behavior issues and died in the state institution in 1951, a month before I was born. His twin also seems to have had mental deficits and couldn't make much of a living. Leila's elder sister, Annie, liked to play with dolls with Karen. She married several times and died young with no surviving children.

Charles Cox was a US Army veteran and had a successful, middle-class life as a farmer and insurance salesman. He was a stable husband and father to Ruth and Linda and took on the care of Karen and his parents. When they went into mental decline, Frank and Corrie moved into a trailer at the back of Charlie's property. Karen told me that Charlie and Ruth persisted in their attempts to adopt her, "and raise me with Linda, but Momma refused."

In one of our first phone conversations, Karen said, "She has low self-esteem. She fixates on the TV with anything about adoption when birth mothers come from behind the curtain and meet the child they gave up. Momma never let on." Leila didn't have the wherewithal to search.

Leila died in August 1994, one year after our reunion. Her heart and kidneys failed her at age sixty-eight. Karen and I were among the few at her graveside, mourning our mutual loss: the mother I had only lately met and Karen's loss of a momma who couldn't stay put. We mourned for Leila's broken heart, all the losses she suffered by consequence of her birth and upbringing through no fault of her own, by her neglect or by conscious choice. In the end, all was forgiven.

After Momma died, Karen and I continued our conversations about ancestral connections and explored three churchyards for clues. I think I speak for us both when I say that we felt a genuine peace in walking among the antique gravestones of Antioch, Standing Springs, and Rocky Creek. They were strolls of exploration and discovery, finding meaning in our shared past.

We contacted a few area Hendersons, because Karen recalled a man by that name had come to visit the Roper Mountain farmhouse when she was very young. He gave her a baby doll. Grandma's brother, Arthur, was most likely the visitor rather than Momma's first husband who had the same surname. (Henderson is a fairly common North and South Carolina name of Welsh origin.) Leila could not, or would not, reveal my biological father's name, and there were no known photos, so I thought myself powerless to continue the search for my paternity. At my first contact with Catholic Charities in 1990 when I received nonidentifying information, the agency worker said my birth mother had "insisted" she didn't know who fathered me. Leila told me too, "I don't remember," and I now believe her. Sadly, my biological father was inconsequential to her and her pregnancy with me an unwanted accident. I might have had an inkling then that Momma's life bore no semblance of romance, but I wanted to believe in her love.

After I found Leila and traced my Cox and Lenderman sides, I was cautiously optimistic that I could ask for and receive my original birth certificate and other pre-adoption records. Although I knew in my gut that Momma didn't know who he was, I wrote to Catholic Charities and Marie Lescord that I had been welcomed by my birth mother, half-sister, and other close family members, and I asked for information about my biological father. Marie never responded.

I laid aside my quest for paternity to pursue a new gardening career and take responsibility for my widowed Mom and Nana, who'd lived in California since the late 1970s. I sold or packed their furniture for the movers, put their home on the market, and brought my aged loved ones back to Pennsylvania.

The unexpected and dire happened. At age fifty-seven, I survived a devastating brain bleed, a life-changing ordeal for Phil and me. I was in rehabilitation for two solid years, and am still disabled. I've devoted myself to writing—forced to give up gardening.

Adoptees had been using Ancestry DNA tests as a discovery tool, and I dipped my toe in genealogy about seven years ago. My early genetic matches pointed to the ancestral lines I'd claimed during two Lenderman-Cox reunions.

Karen was willing to test too, and we saw the measure of our genetic linkage in centimorgans, and I worked on our maternal family tree.

6. Lottie

On Valentine's Day 2015, Karen and I were stunned to learn that Leila could have shared much more with us. Karen stumbled across a South Carolina internet message board post from 2007 by a woman who had been searching for her mother, Leila Grace Cox, for years. Here is an excerpt.

> *I am Lottie Lee C., and my grandmother was Lottie Lee C. C. I am the daughter of her son, Alonzo Lanneau C.…My father, grandmother, and grandfather are buried at Providence Baptist Church in Macedonia South Carolina…*
> *My grandmother died before my birth, so I never had the opportunity to meet her…My father, Alonzo, died when I was four years old, and my mother Leila Grace Cox C. left us when I was six weeks old…my grandfather, Andrew, raised me until his death…I have been searching for my birth mother…I have always lived in South Carolina…Lottie*

It was like a thunderbolt! Karen's and my excitement stung as we realized that Leila had lied by not telling us about our younger sister. I emailed Lottie after our first phone call, surprising myself with my ease of familiarity. The experience of my first phone call with my other maternal half-sister was my initiation into the life of biological sisterhood. What follows is a series of emails between Karen, Lottie, and myself after my first phone call to Lottie.

> Me: *Lottie, The short version is that I contacted Catholic Charities, Charleston, since I had my adoption papers. They would only give me non-identifying information, and it was very sketchy. With the name Lee—the papers referred to me as Ruth Ann—I pursued a path for Lee's for months. This was in 1992 before the internet was widely in use. I got the help of local genealogists. The break came when a Catholic Charities agent offered to give me more information for a fee. She would only give it to me on the phone. I wrote the extra information she revealed to me on the surface of a manila envelope. I learned our mother's name, Leila Grace Cox. I later learned that Lee was the name of her divorced husband. Karn was the name the adoption worker read me, which gave me no clue as to the sex of our sibling. I guess the name was interpreted from Momma's speech. For more weeks I phoned, wrote letters to agencies and the genealogist who used old cemetery records, maps, and phone directories, this time with the name Cox. It all led to my call to Lawrence Cox, our now sweet, deceased cousin, who shared information with me. First, he gave me the number of Aunt Ruth Cox, Momma's sister-in-law, and she gave me Karen's number. Never give up asking, dear Lottie! xo*
>
> Lottie: *WOW—you did all this before the internet!! You are very strong willed. What happened when you first met our mom? Did she ever say anything to you about what happened?*

Me: *Karen told me that at first, Leila denied that the woman who called Karen was a daughter but soon gave in to Karen's insistence. She had me in St. Francis hospital, and she left me. St. Francis was affiliated with the Philip's Mercy Hospital and Infant Home in Rock Hill, where I was taken.*

Although we did have a great reunion, there were a lot of mixed feelings. I think our mother's poor health and lifestyle contributed to her confusion. She had end-stage kidney failure, was on dialysis, and while still in TX, where she had lived for 32 years, her leg was amputated. But we got around in SC, went to cemeteries in Greenville to visit ancestors' graves and a Lenderman-Cox reunion. It was often pleasant but sometimes strained. When I returned to PA, she called me often. After one very early morning call, I had to set up boundaries. She was very apologetic and seemed embarrassed. The honeymoon period had an urgency to her. She knew it would be short lived.

Lottie: *I was born in Berkeley County Memorial Hospital in Moncks Corner. I went to Family Court a few years back in Berkeley County to get a copy of my original birth certificate. When I asked for it, the clerk laughed and said South Carolina was a sealed state. Therefore, the only way I could get a copy was to hire an attorney. I still remember how she laughed without even caring how it affected me.*

Karen: *I am so excited to meet you! I live near Spartanburg where my dad's family is from. Momma brought me here when I was 13, and it was the best thing she could have done for me. I was able to finish school, marry, have 3 children, Barbara, Daniel, and Joshua, and 4 grandchildren. I have lived a fairly stable life despite Momma's mixed-up life. Mary Ellen found me 22 years ago, and now we've found you. I can hardly wait to meet you! I truly believe God set all of this in motion. Please call me when you can. xx*

Lottie to Karen and me: *I am so glad that Mary Ellen did not give up the search. I have always prayed that this would happen. I always had a void in my life wondering where my mom was and if she ever thought of me.*

I was named after my father's mother, who died too early! Like you, I was raised by my grandparents. I was always the apple of my grandfather's eye and was always by his side. He passed when I was 8. My step-grandmother could no longer care for me because of her age. The aunts and uncles considered placing me in an orphanage, but my uncle Leroy and his wife took me in and then adopted me. I dearly loved my uncle Leroy, but his wife was not good to me. Many unhappy years. I am so happy to have you in my life now.

Love and hugs to you,
Lottie

Part Sixteen

Sisterhood

Years had passed since the first night of our reunion when Karen and I talked in our beds long into the night. She had shared stories that connected us as sisters. Karen now shared, by email to Lottie and me, a darker story of neglect, desperation, and anger:

She came and got me and took me to Texas when I was ten, where she was living with her husband, Frank Adams, and their daughter, Susan Paulette (Susie). It was terrible! He was an alcoholic, and she drank too. Then they would fight. She was a mean, crying drunk. He was abusive to me too. At 13, she brought me back to SC. She was going to leave me with her parents again, but by then Grandma had dementia, so we left for Charleston on a Greyhound. Momma never drove. We stayed about a week in an old hotel I think on King St. She had lived there before and knew the owners. She took the last of her money and bought a white blouse and a black skirt, her uniform at her new job, where she had worked in the past. But Momma was very heavy, and her looks were shot. She was leaving Susie and me alone in the room at night while she worked. That wasn't working, so we hitchhiked to Spartanburg, and she asked my daddy, Ralph Lee, if he would take me. He said yes, so I stayed, and she and Susie went back to Texas. I finished school in 1966.

Our half-sister, Susan, had a seizure disorder, thought to have been from birth, maybe because she was a large "diabetic baby." I had read in my adoptive mother's notes that I was nine pounds six ounces at birth, a possible sign of my mother's incipient type II diabetes. Karen told me that Leila was protective, and breastfed Susan for a couple of years, but things went downhill for the family with Leila and her husband's drinking, transience, low income—Frank was working in a filling station—and general neglect. Susan drowned at age sixteen in a creek at a friend's family picnic. Frank and Leila were not on-site, and Frank was called to identify his child's body. The police report noted there was difficulty determining who had called in the emergency, and that a man who attempted to rescue Susan also drowned in the rough water. Leila's life was immersed in loss.

We three saw the uncomfortable truth about our birth mother. Since Lottie had lived all her life in Charleston, might Leila have tried to contact her—if not when she briefly stayed in Charleston when Karen was ten, why not when we reunited at the end of Leila's life? We could have all known the joy of reunion. When she came up against her lifetime of the unforeseen and unplanned, she was incapable of making clear choices, and let things slide. Maybe she was overwhelmed by my surprise contact and couldn't face having left behind her third daughter. Her fear, shame, confusion over the past, and her ill health conspired to let that rare opportunity pass.

The deep wound of relinquishment never goes away, but we need and have a right to know where we are from. Lottie, like myself, didn't know how—or was loathe to ask—the ones who raised her for information, direction, or comfort. We three had struggled with Leila's ghosts all our lives.

February 15, 2015

Karen: *Subject: Hello! We're glad we found you!*

Daniel and I were speaking of her the other night. He remembers that time as not a good time when she came here, and he said he never felt any connection with her. It was so hard suddenly putting her in a growing family, especially teenage boys. Looking back, she probably should have gone into a nursing home because she wasn't going to be happy anywhere, because she wasn't happy in her own heart. And of course, now, we know why. Love, Karen

Lottie to Karen and me: *Never second guess what you gave her, Karen. It was meant to be. You gave her love even in the end. I could not imagine you doing anything else. That is who you are and why Mary Ellen and I love you so much! Lottie*

Sometime later, I wrote to Karen and Lottie:

Who the man was that fathered me is the mystery. Momma's comings and goings make it difficult. Could he be any of the 3 men she was closest to? If we do go the DNA route, the best bet to linking a father would be by working with the 3 of us. I'm checked in with the Search Squad on Facebook. They are a team. I think most of them are women genealogists, investigators, and search angels. I gave them the info I could, and we'll see what they come up with! Love you lots, M. E.

Lottie agreed to test. Weeks later, I forwarded the AncestryDNA notice to my sisters:

Mon, May 25, 2015
Great news! Your results are in.
SISTERS!

From Karen

To: Lottie and Mary Ellen
Oh boy, Lottie, truly you are now in the crazy kinship
of Mary Ellen and Karen! I'm so happy. You are one
of us forever and ever!!

When my elder sister and I found each other, we spent hours poking around the churchyards upstate and in Greenville. We were happy to repeat this ritual when we connected with Lottie for the first time, discovering each other and many ancestral graves. We visited the streets where Frank and Corrie lived near the mill where Momma and her father once worked. We all were validated of our common ancestry.

Part Seventeen

The Dad I Never Had

I was determined to identify my birth father. I visited a DNA search Facebook group frequently and came upon a post by a man who, he and I were astonished to see, was in St. Philip's Mercy Hospital and Infant Home at the same time! His name is Joe C., born in August 1951, a month before me, also in St. Francis Hospital in Greenville. We had been fellow "crib mates" as adoptees sometimes refer to each other, or institutional "inmates," and through Catholic Charities were both adopted by Air Force couples stationed at Shaw. His guardian ad litem was Sister Mathia, and his adoption was handled by the same Rock Hill law firm as mine. What serendipity to learn that he was living an hour away in southwest Florida! We visited a few times, compared our adoption papers and certificates of baptism and adoption, and remain connected by email and Facebook. It was a smooth process for "eligible" relinquished newborns in South Carolina in those days, and I imagine it's at least as swift today through Catholic Charities and other adoption venues. That Joe and I went through the system and grew up in Air Force families was an extraordinary coincidence.

Joe had petitioned York County SC Court for his original birth certificate but was only able to view his documents in person. Several years have passed, and there has been some activity in the South Carolina legislature to open adoptees' records, but the outcome is less than satisfactory. They remain under the state seal. People like Joe and me, and many hundreds of other adoptees, are speaking out for our right to equal access to our original birth records. Joe referred me to the office of the director of Social Ministry and Catholic Charities in Charleston, and I sent an email request for information about my birth father in May 2015.

Dear Ms. M:

In my 40's, I was able to find my birth mother, Leila Grace Cox, 1/2 sister Karen Lane Lee, as well as cousins, and learned about an array of maternal ancestors, in 1994—much to our joy and happiness—all without benefit of the internet. During the past 20 or so years, I have suffered a major stroke at 58, and our birth mother and other kin have died. It is surely possible that my birth father is not still living, but I would be happy to know his name, and my paternal heritage..."

As you see, there are still some unanswered questions. My sincere hope is that additional identifying information can be given to me along the lines of the form below.

Sincere thanks,
Mary Ellen Gambutti

Questions I have regarding my natural father:

1. *Age and date of birth*
2. *Name at time of my birth*
3. *Height*
4. *Weight*
5. *Hair color*
6. *Eye color*
7. *Education*
8. *Religious background*
9. *Socioeconomic background*
10. *Ethnic origins (for example, mother Irish/English, father Italian/Italian)*
11. *Number and ages and sex of siblings he had (cause of death if deceased)*
12. *Where he was born*
13. *Where he lived at the time of my birth*
14. *Marital status*
15. *His usual occupation*
16. *His parents' ages and ethnic origins (for example, mother Irish/English, father Italian/Italian)*
17. *His parents' educational background*
18. *His parents' physical descriptions*
19. *His parents' usual occupations*
20. *If his parents were deceased, age and year they died and cause of death*
21. *Any other non-identifying information (hobbies, talents, interests, etc.)*

I am hereby requesting the complete medical histories of my natural mother, natural father, and their families.

I am requesting that you examine my file to deter-
mine whether or not my natural mother and/or father
placed on file a consent form granting permission to
disclose the information contained in my original birth
certificate or any other identifying or non-identifying
information about my natural mother and/or father.

Hi Ms. Gambutti,

I would be more than happy to help you. But, in order
for me to do so, you would have to fill out a Reunion
Registry packet. The cost for this is $40.00. If you
would like to continue, please let me know and I will
send the packet.

I gave the go-ahead to her to send me the packet, but didn't send the additional money for paternal nonidentifying information. I was convinced it would not produce results, when I read the packet, a portion of which is here:

* *Was I their first child?*
* *Any full siblings?*
* *Any half-siblings on my father's side?*
* *The first name of each birth parent:*
* *Where was each birth parent born?*
* *Did they reside in __ (insert city and state in which you, the Adoptee, were born)?*
* *If answered "no," were they from (put your state)?*
* *Were they from another state and came to/for my delivery and adoption?*

- *I am hereby requesting the complete medical histories of my natural mother, natural father, and their families.*
- *Please list any/all childhood diseases or surgeries known for each birth parent:*
- *Please list any/all genetic disorders known for each birth parent:*
- *Please list any/all known diseases or illnesses experienced by each birth parent:*
- *Were any of these diseases or illnesses experienced during my birth mother's pregnancy with me?*
- *Were either birth parents exposed to German measles, polio, or tuberculosis during the pregnancy?*
- *At the time of my adoption were my birth grandparents still living?*
- *If not, what did they die from?*
- *What were their names?*
- *At the time of my adoption were my birth great-grandparents still living?*
- *If not, what did they die from?*
- *What were their names?*
- *[Include your name and address here]:*
- *Please include any medical records and/or information known for each birth parent. Please include any medical records, birth records, nursery log records of my birth, and any known subsequent medical treatment before adoption:*
- *Name and address of the medical facility where treatment was administered:*
- *Name and address of my delivery doctor:*
- *Name and address of the attending pediatrician:*

*Thank you for your courtesy in providing me with the
requested information.*

*Sincerely,
[Your signature]*

I had no further contact with Ms. M.

~

I didn't have a regional accent—was never in one place long
enough to develop one—I would take on the persona of a
new acquaintance so she would accept me. I had no related
cousins or siblings, and I didn't see myself in my immediate
family. Finding an identity took work when no one looked
like me. It was a preoccupation, a necessity, and with no
voice associations, I had to scrutinize their way of talking
to make it mine. Otherwise, how should I talk or act?

This was a chore, my job in a constantly changing sphere of
friends, to be vigilant in order to assimilate. I had no physical
mirrors until my daughter was born when I was twenty, and
then the realization hit me. *There had been no one else!* I might
have noticed this work, this habit, around then, thinking it a
social skill. I must have done it through school, this self-preservation mechanism to make me safe with strangers. Sometimes
the exposure wasn't long enough to make the mirror work
when we left again, but when there was time, I could act like,
talk like, be like—be accepted. *Who else could I be?*

In Facebook DNA search groups, I was encouraged to
test my maternal half-sisters on AncestryDNA to construe,
by manipulating matches, who my genetic father and family
were. Karen, Lottie, and I were pretty sure we had different
fathers. I was the daughter still lacking my full picture.

A genetic genealogist, Rick K., whom I located through a Facebook group, assisted me in cobbling together a test family tree derived from a second cousin match. Sherry B. and I developed close communication, and she was most generous in sharing common ancestral clues from her tree. Her family roots were in Georgia near the South Carolina border. The genealogist suggested that DNA "hints" that didn't correspond with Karen's and Lottie's could be assumed matches from my paternal side. He coached me to extend this test tree far and wide in the hope that new close matches would appear.

It was a brilliant strategy that allowed me to dream of the possibilities of my roots and origins. It helped me open inquiries with fellow Ancestry users willing to shed light on our possible family connections. In return, I was able to share what I had found. I was even able to help a few distant kin to manage their DNA tests. This remarkable experience broadened not only my search for paternity but my ethnic and historical horizons.

One of the highlights of this project was the moment when I wandered among family trees in my Georgia ancestral places, close to the South Carolina border near Greenville. Assuming I was conceived after a casual or one-night stand with my birth mother, I admit to a sense of embarrassment as I knocked on people's virtual doors, seeking a paternal match. Though I had learned to combat the shame of my illegitimacy, or my embarrassment for her when I met my mother's family in the 1990s, the discomfort resurfaced when I searched for my father. It was a stab in the dark.

This man looked something like me, and his family tree was nearby. I explored the possibility and mulled over making contact with his daughter by email. She was kind and understanding of my plight. Several years younger than I, she shared what she knew about her father's families, which wasn't a great deal. I asked her to do a sibling DNA test with me—not available through Ancestry.com—and she obliged, though she felt sure her father had not been unfaithful to her mother. But the cynic in me thought, *he was a navy man, and my mother was "loose"!*

It required some planning to obtain and transfer the samples with the platform that was exclusively for sibling tests, as she worked as a nurse missionary in East Asia. I had her test medium sent to her, and she enlisted a colleague to carry her saliva specimen back to the United States and mail it to the lab in-country where it would be run against my waiting sample. The anticipation and logistics were exciting but turned out to be unfruitful. I wondered if my new friend breathed a sigh of relief.

I skirted my paternal family without realizing it. A few third-cousin matches were circumspect, not recognizing my haphazard "lines." The stigma of illegitimacy stuck. I fondly remember my cousin, Lawrence Cox, who lovingly put the baggage of my kinship aside to embrace me into my maternal side of the family.

A line of Smiths was promising, a distance away from Susan's kin, but not by much. The rich photo galleries of some families made me long for the connections. They were distant family, after all. I was giddily determined; the exercise was close to the satisfaction it could someday reap.

Three years ago, after more than a year of research in Ancestry, a first-cousin match with the initials J. G. appeared. *My time and effort might pay off!* I invested yet more time sleuthing on Facebook for potential names to go with the initials, names that matched locations.

I contacted D. Gunter, hoping he would be the son of my close match, J. G. What a relief when he said, "Yes, that's my dad!" J. G.—Jack Gunter, and his wife, Nancy, had taken DNA tests but never connected to trees or followed matches. Nancy coincidentally appeared as a distant match to me on my maternal side—N. G.—Nancy Rogers Gunter.

I accomplished with DNA testing what I had all but given up on. What a feeling to chat with a newly found cousin—my closest paternal DNA match to date! Jack and Nancy had a hunch about my paternal connection. Jack's mother, Janie Lee Thrasher Gunter, who died in 2002, was the wife of George Manning Gunter. Janie's brother, Andrew Larkin Thrasher Jr., could be my biological father. His age and lifestyle profiled him. He could have had a liaison with my mother around 1950–1951.

Junior, as Andrew Larkin Thrasher was called, died in August 1973 in Anderson, South Carolina, when I was almost twenty-two and my baby girl was a year old. He was a World War II Army veteran, born in February 1930 in Anderson. He was a heavy drinker and smoker and worked as a household pesticide applicator. It seemed all but certain that this was the man.

Cousin D. Gunter typed out his close family on Facebook Messenger, and I transcribed them into my family tree, finding the hint for Andrew Larkin Thrasher Jr., connecting him to Leila Cox as "partner" and me as a daughter. I connected with four paternal half-siblings the next day—all around my age—Libby, Teri, George, and Carol. Libby, Andrew's first daughter, was born on April 1, 1951, and I was born that September.

Andrew Larkin Thrasher Junior was the father I never had. What if I hadn't been adopted by a military officer, an ex-seminarian, into a strict Catholic household? What if I hadn't been raised by a father who was often absent, distracted, sometimes harsh—abusive at his worst—but who also professed his devotion to his wife and protected his family the way he was taught?

Junior showed that he wasn't much of a dad to my half-siblings. He was devoted to drinking more than to their mother.

Libby's message to me:

I did not see my dad until I was eleven years old. My mom brought us to visit my Aunt. Then he passed when I was eighteen (of lung cancer), so I didn't know him that well. He was raised in Anderson, SC. She was raised in Tampa. They were married in Greenville, SC. My dad was an alcoholic. He and Mom separated in 1955. She moved back to Tampa.

Junior, your genes are expressed in my face, my eyes in mirth and sadness, our cheeks and length of face. *Did you know? Did she tell you?* We never saw each other's photos—nothing to be proud of, nothing to compare our mirrored images. Not until I was in my sixties did I see your faded photo. *Your other children are my family by half, and I didn't know them. You hardly knew them.*

I finally found the wealth of family in six living half-siblings. I was fortunate to spend a year with my birth mother. No siblings on my paternal side are known to be deceased, and we know of only one of Leila's children to have died young.

Mary Ellen Gambutti

I consider my search for kin a big success.

I've celebrated my South Carolina kinship many times since 1993. I've been with my paternal siblings, cousins, nieces, and nephews several times when my husband and I traveled between Florida and Pennsylvania during the years Mom lived in a nursing home.

In summer of 2021, as my husband and I drove through South Carolina on our way to our new home in Delaware, we visited with my Gunter cousins. I always appreciate their warm, unpretentious company. During this visit, I spent time with my younger sister, Teri. We decided through sharing photos that we look the most alike and most like our father in hair, eyes, and features. We see how I "favor" our grandmother, Annie Grace Addison Thrasher, at this age. I wonder how it would have been to sit with her and chat as I did with my nana. I helped our sister, Carol, test through Ancestry, and the match is undeniable. We Thrasher sisters bear similarities in coloring, voice, and frame, while George has the eyes, hair color, and a rugged appearance, perhaps like other men in our ancestral line. I plan to continue to trace my ancestral origins in the British Isles.

Part Eighteen

Appealing for Pre-Adoption Records

I first connected with the lady I'll call J. in Catholic Charities in Charleston in September 2021, with a request for my birth and foster care records, making my strongest plea to date. After some difficulty locating my file, she did find it under my adoptive parents' name.

Good morning, Ma'am,

I finally found the file – I'm so glad you absolutely knew that it was here.

I do want to let you know that there has been nothing new placed in your file since the last time you received information in 1992. I would be more than happy to fill out another non-identifying information report for you, but I don't believe anything has changed since your first request.

Unfortunately, the adoption files are still closed in the state of SC–I included the link below to the state website (particularly section 63-9-780): https://www.scstatehouse.gov/code/t63c009.php

If you would like me to proceed with gathering the non-identifying information, please fill out the attached

documents and send back at your earliest convenience.
Thank you again for your patience!

I replied to J. with the written letters exchanged between me and the adoption worker in 1992, who had given me my non-identifying information—without a form request. Now, having details from my searches, I informed her that all concerned parties—my adoptive parents, birth mother, and bio father—are deceased.

She replied:

Unfortunately, the adoption files are still closed in the state of SC–I included the link below to the state website (particularly section 63-9-780): https://www.scstatehouse.gov/code/t63c009.php.

If you would like me to proceed with gathering the non-identifying information, please fill out the attached documents and send back at your earliest convenience.

Thank you again for your patience!
Sincerely
J.

And

I just wanted to follow-up with you to let you know that I'm still waiting on a response from the Office of Vital Records at DHEC. Once I hear back from them, I'll get in touch with you.

Thank you,
J.

Dec. 17, 2021
Dear J.

I want to touch base with you to reaffirm my need for Catholic Charities agency records, including records from my pre-adoption. As you know, my adoptive parents, the Caffrey's, are both dead, as are my biological mother Leila Grace Cox and my bio father Andrew Larkin Thrasher. I have been in successful reunion with both my maternal and paternal sides; maternal since 1994, and paternal since 2017.

I am aware that Rep. Hays has the adoption bill in Judiciary until the new session opens. I pray they will have the compassion and good sense to forward a good clean bill that addresses the civil rights of adoptees.

I am attaching several snippets that should be of interest to Vital Records. I understand that they have not yet gotten back to you with a decision to forward my records.

The letter from Catholic Charities to my parents is the announcement that I (Baby Ruth Ann) is available to them in Rock Hill, and other details.

The snips from my mother Agnes's baby book indicate in pencil the date "11-13-51 admitted." I want to know where I was from the time I was born 9/21/51 in St. Francis Hospital, Greenville until that date. Was it my admission to the "Annex" of St Philip's Mercy Hospital, which was the Infant and Children's home? If not, where was I for six weeks? I'd like the history. The next snippet is my mother's note, with a blank line of "where," which states my birth was in York County. My mother thought this, but it was not factual. Until I was 40, I thought I was born in Rock Hill, as per my Certificate of Baptism and Birth, which was a falsification. Dr. Bratton is a name that appears nowhere else, but he did not attend my birth. I was born in St. Francis my birth mother told me. Sr. Francella was the baby nurse when Mom and Dad picked me up. Sr. Mathia was the administrator of the hospital and infant home, as well as my guardian ad litem, and Catholic Charities liaison.

Please feel free to share this letter and the attachments to whomever, including Vital Statistics. I have the full court record, and adoption decree.

Please let me have my full birth record, and notes from Catholic Charities. I'd like of course, to see my birth certificate, but a photo would be just as good. I am 70 and a stroke survivor. I don't want to petition the court if I don't have to.

Sincerely,
Mary Ellen.

I was encouraged by her cheery reply.

Dec 20, 2021
Good afternoon, Ma'am!

I apologize for the delay – I am still waiting to hear back from DHEC regarding the legality of handing over your adoption record. I am in the process now of trying to locate an attorney who can possibly help me with those questions.

I fully understand how important this is to you, so I am diligently working on finding the answer. Thank you so much for your patience.

Sincerely,
J.

~

Jan. 10, 2022
Good afternoon, Ma'am!

I hope this email finds you well, and I'd like to thank you for your patience as I went through the proper channels to find an answer for you.

I finally spoke to an Adoption Attorney and was told that in South Carolina the only way to open an adoption file is with a court order.

However, it is highly unlikely that the court would grant access to an adoption file unless there is a severe, life threatening illness that the adoptee has.

The majority of what is in your file pertains to your adopted parents and the documents they provided in order for the adoption to be granted.

There is nothing new or different from what you received in 1992 when you were corresponding with Catholic Charities.

As far as an original birth certificate, the attorney mentioned going through the state registrar's office if you would like to get a copy of that – that is not in your file here at Catholic Charities.

Again, thank you for your patience, and I'm sorry I didn't have more useful information for you.

If you have any other questions, please don't hesitate to contact me.

Thank you…

J.

~

New South Carolina Adoption Law

On May 16, South Carolina Governor McMaster signed into law H5000 that allows persons age eighteen or over who were adopted in the state to request a copy of their original birth certificate, regardless of the date their adoption was finalized. A biological parent must consent to the release of the Original Birth Certificate, or the adoptee must prove that the biological parent(s) is deceased. The new adoption law takes effect on May 16, 2023.

In the weeks prior, I wrote to Judiciary Committee members, asking them to let the bill introduced by Representative R.J. May die. I urged them to start over with an unrestrictive bill in the next session. Although the result is a flawed, restrictive law, I intend to pursue my Original Birth Certificate. My biological mother did not disclose my father, but I will soon have my mother's death certificate.

Adoptee's United on the new law:

https://adopteesunited.org/legislation/state/#sc:~:text=H5000%20is%20essentially,May%2016%2C%202023

~

Part Nineteen

Wayward

You might say she was wayward. Unstable. When she knew the baby's father, she married him, then quickly divorced him. At sixteen, she married a man in his thirties to escape her confining, rural home life. How many children did Leila Grace Cox have?

In September 2012, Karen wrote:

I told you about my memory of pieces of conversations about twins, and since Lottie has memories too, I think it may have happened. I can remember as a child hearing Grandma and someone talking, and it must have imprinted in my brain about twins.

From Lottie:

Gertrude was my birth Dad's sister. She managed several bars throughout Charleston-North Charleston during her working years. I am sure that is how my birth dad met Momma in the bars of Charleston and North Charleston. Once Momma became pregnant with me and Dad married her, Aunt Gertrude became more involved. I am sure Aunt Gertrude was the one that told her sister Aunt Maggie that Momma had twins after she left my birth dad, so I am assuming Aunt Gertrude kept in touch with Momma. Momma probably continued hanging in the Charleston-North Charleston bars as the naval shipyard was still active with sailors coming in and out of Charleston. Of course, sailors love bars, and that is where Momma hung out, trying to make a dollar. I asked my Aunt Aileen once, "How did Dad meet Mom?" She said, "Probably in one of those bars in Charleston where Lawton (Dad's brother) and Alonzo (birth dad) would hang out. Those from my dad's family that knew Mom have passed on, taking with them all the family secrets. I did not begin asking questions until later in my life. And then, I did not ask enough questions. I was always afraid to talk about her.

Two industries created jobs in North Charleston while Mom was living. During my young life, I remember Aunt Gertrude managing a bar in the old village of North Charleston. Afterward, she managed a bar on Rivers Avenue called The Hideaway. Many women worked at the Garco Mill...those that didn't hang in the bars servicing the sailors. Unfortunately, Mom did the latter. The women of the night would hang out at the bars waiting for the sailors to depart from the ships. Also, when the civilian men that were workers at the shipyard and Garco Mill were paid, the bars filled up. Back then, the prostitutes could walk the streets without worry of arrest. What a life!

I shared with my sisters an email Karen sent me in 2015:

> *I remember going to Charleston with Uncle Charlie and Aunt Ruth. They wanted to adopt me, but Momma would have no part of it. Aunt Ruth told me later that she was pregnant because Charlie said "You've got yourself in trouble again." I remember it was cold because we walked on the beach--winter. I must have been eight because I was living with them. If this was in 1956, she may have been pregnant with "the twins."*

I was born in 1951, Lottie in 1954, and Karen in 1948. Twin boys were born to Leila's parents--Wilton had survived.
From Lottie:

> *My family always said I would probably have twins, and now I know that twins were on Mom's side and my Dad's side. In fact, both my grandparents had twin siblings.*

Leila abandoned Lottie to her father at six weeks. Where was Momma in 1955 and 1956? Did she go back to Greenville to give birth? She might have stayed with a friend in Charleston—we just don't know. As Karen had said, "She came and went."
From Lottie:

> *Hospitals in Charleston at that time were Roper Hospital, Bon Secours St. Francis Hospital, Baker Hospital, and Charleston County Memorial Hospital. Baker Hospital is now closed, Bon Secours*

St. Francis merged with Roper and is now Roper/ St Francis, Charleston County Memorial Hospital is closed, and Medical University Hospital of South Carolina may have been active then...not sure. The Charleston County Memorial Hospital took indigent care patients at that time. Unless the twins' family paid for her to deliver at one of the private hospitals, I would think she would have used Bon Secours St. Francis Hospital in Charleston, since she had used the sisters' services with you, Mary Ellen.

From me:

Yes, it would make sense that she would use St. Francis since she was familiar with St. Francis Hospital in Greenville—their willingness to take indigent mothers. Could we find a record of live birth? Since we have tested DNA, if other children of Leila's—either of the twins should test—they would come up as maternal matches to us.

On May 29, 2022, I read a new message in Ancestry from someone I'll call C.:

Hello! After receiving my DNA results you came up as one of my cousins. I am trying to find both my mom and dad's biological families they were both adopted as babies and they have never tried to find their biological parents. Anyway, write me back if you want to chat.

My reply:

> *It looks like you are a close match on my maternal side. I am adopted and searched years ago, finding my birth mother in Greenville, SC. My 1/2 sisters are Karen and Lottie...*

A *"close match"* on Ancestry might make her a half-sister. Could this 1st cousin/half-niece match be the daughter of our brother?

C.'s Reply:

> *I can tell you his adoptive name...*

Her stories unraveled in a frenzy; in the wildness of discovery. Intense curiosity, like we three sisters the day we were introduced through a wi-fi connection, between we four Cox ancestors. But the elation of kinship discovery is dampened by our half-brother's unfortunate history, which precludes his inclusion in our call, and the likelihood of some future communication with him. His long criminal record for theft pales against his violent and predatory past. We have seen the reports. Our niece told us her mother separated from him when she and her biological brother were young children.

We found a "bio" screenshot he'd saved in his photos; it reads like a testament to his instability with full stops after every word. He states he was born in Baker Psychiatric Hospital in Charleston, SC July 1955, and the Jewish couple who adopted him, his marriage, and his children's names. His self-images reveal an ill individual with a flat affect.

Lottie writes:

June 14, 2022

WOW! I am so amazed that this was posted. My grandparents lived on the other side of Colonial Lake I think before I was born. It was my step grandmothers home. The hospital is still there but was transformed into condos a few years ago.

That really explains why Moma gave so many babies away. She was not mentally able to be a Mother. There was no help for women born in poverty during that time in their life. She could have been treated and lived a normal life. Instead, she made bad decisions and did what it took to survive. Mental illness is complex. I am so glad that I had family members that took me in and loved me when I was growing up. Those years with my grandparents molded me into who I am today. How do we go about getting those hospital records?

My reply:

...this goes against the idea of a Catholic Charities adoption...the adoption could have been brokered within their Jewish community. C. recalls her mother or another adult saying that he was born in a psychiatric hospital. If she did have mental issues, which I believe she did, and so does Lottie, it's possible Lottie's abandonment at 6 weeks might have been triggered by postpartum psychosis. She possibly then hooked up with someone, or was raped, and had a breakdown. It's possible she was on the street, or in a hotel something like where she waitressed. Karen had told

the story about her leaving with Susie and her by bus
from TX and staying in a room, I guess above a bar?
It may have been one of Gertrude's bars...

Karen reminded us that Leila had revealed two suicidal episodes. When she married to Ralph in Biloxi, MS, and was pregnant with Karen, she had her head in the gas oven and had to be pulled away. At a later time, she was rescued when she tried to jump from the bridge over Greenville's Reedy River. Was she pregnant with me at the time? I was born in 1951 in Greenville. Discovery is not always pretty. Leila bears a striking; almost alarming resemblance to him in photos in her twenties and older. We showed C. old photos of Frank, our grandfather, Uncle Charlie, and Aunt Annie Cox. All share the large frame, heavy build, and barrel-chested, strong upper body; facial similarities, and head shape as Leila and her son.

We were shocked to learn that our half-brother is epileptic; a family trait shared with Leila's daughter, Susan, and her brother, Wilton. What Karen remembers about Uncle Wilton: *He got hit by a car driven by the mill boss, broke his leg, and never healed right. He was mentally challenged and lived at home. Got accused of rape by a woman in the neighborhood. That's when he got sent to live at the state hospital for a few years til he died in 1951.*

The record shows our brother had a lengthy sentence, and upon release was sent to a mental hospital. With no record yet available, we can guess that since he lived in Columbia then, it was likely the same State hospital where Wilton died.

The need to know is strong and natural. Even if my birth mother's liaison with my bio father was a one-time occasion, I'm happy to have found her and to know both my natural families. The knowledge of my out-of-wedlock birth hasn't deterred me from finding the whole story. I learned that the truth isn't always pretty, but it is vital in the quest for identity.

Would I have searched for my birth mother had I known about her lifestyle? In my early forties, it would not have stopped me in my tracks. I would not have been put off by the stigma of the loose woman. I wasn't embarrassed—one of the justifications for sealing birth records. I hoped the cousins I called in those first fraught days would not be put off by an unknown adoptee seeking family out of the blue, and I'll always be grateful to Cousin Lawrence for his kindness and immediate acceptance, and to my sister, Karen, for believing and supporting me.

Part Twenty

The Parents I Had

"Reconciliation brings something new into the lives of the reconciled. [It]…removes our fears…by disarming the ghosts of the past. It substitutes plain human faces for fancies…reconciliation."

—Jean Paton,
Orphan Journey

Letter to Mom's Memory

Mom and I kept up a sporadic correspondence during the twenty-seven years they lived in California—first cards and letters, and eventually email. I've saved many of the handwritten ones.

Dear Mom,

I feel sure all the Air Force moves and Dad's transitions were hard for you, Mom. I only remember seeing you cry once or twice. Once, when Dad returned from Iceland, he was yelling at you for not getting rid of things you had saved. You were weeping for your lost memories, for the many things you had already left behind in moves. *My four-year-old self felt sad for you as I peered around your bedroom door.*

There must have been heartache over many losses, foremost, the loss of biological motherhood and mourning the child you couldn't have. You might have suffered from regret around your choice to adopt an unknown child to make the family you and Dad otherwise would not have had. Although we never spoke about it directly, it was palpable to me.

We both had our strengths and weaknesses. We are not mirrors of each other. I studied every move you made, particularly as a young child. You were my world, though so different physically and in manner. When I was a teen, our physical differences became more apparent, pronounced. My identity confusion sharpened. I was nothing like you, a fact you pointed out to me. You sometimes said you wished you weren't well endowed. At your worst, you sometimes mocked me pointing out my gawkiness and lack of grace. Your intent, you inferred, was to see me improve. Did you resent me?

You wanted to toughen me up. "It's just your imagination!" and "Don't be so sensitive." When I trembled in a panic—a panic that would recur into my thirties—especially with the fear of getting sick, the episodes could come on like catastrophe. You seemed to ignore symptoms of anxiety and later depression. I wish you had been able to soothe and allay my anxieties. I don't think you meant to be cruel when you said like a prophecy, a prophecy that sounded like a curse, "You'll never be happy!"

I needed your friendship, and when there were no friends or family to be found, I missed those you missed. You took me on errands when Dad wasn't around. Shopping, playing a card game on the floor, taking a ride in the Louisiana countryside. Those were the childhood days I loved you most. I always loved you, Mom, but if you were affectionate, I rarely saw it. I saw your dutifulness, your busyness.

You said, "Actions speak louder than words." I don't remember the words "I love you" until your final years. Through my childhood, you showed your love by sewing my clothes, braiding and curling my hair, keeping me well fed, and keeping house wherever we landed. It was all about practicality: your nurse's training, I think. You were a talented seamstress but never had the time to teach me. You hated to cook and avoided it when we were with Nana since she didn't seem to mind the kitchen. You avoided the garden too, unlike Nana and me who were comfortable and found our solace there. You and I spent many hours alone, together, and with my group of rug hooking friends. You joined us when I brought you back to Pennsylvania, and they loved you too, seeing you the gentle, pleasant old woman who blended well in our group.

I wanted to nurture you in old age. I felt a strong sense of duty and compassion toward you and to Nana—had I learned it from you? My work in healthcare and nursing home activities? I wanted to show you gratitude.

Yours affectionately,
Mary Ellen

Agnes Remembering

On August 10, 2018, Mom's ninety-sixth birthday, her cousin Janet, who was a few years older than me, taped stories in Mom's room at the assisted living center. The words are spoken by Agnes.

Tape clip 1: "Dad's family had a dairy farm in Saltillo, PA. I remember a cave in the hillside where they stored milk and jarred goods. A stream ran through the cave."

Tape clip 2: "Mom, Dad, my brother, Vincent, and I lived in Orbisonia. Vincent was afraid of Dad's horse. Vince had a nightmare the horse was down in the yard eating the dog. Once, Dad brought the horse into the house as a joke. It scared Vince to death. My mom canned fruit in Orbisonia. We lived in the country until I finished first grade. I remember riding to school in a horse-drawn sleigh."

Tape clip 3: "We moved to New York City on West Broadway in the village, when the coal mines closed in 1928. I went to school near Washington Square Park. I jumped rope in the street, played on the roof of Dad's auto repair shop across the street. We moved to West 58th Street, across from Roosevelt Hospital when I started high school. It was nice to live so close to Central Park."

Tape clip 4: "My diary is falling apart. Kept it from 1939–1941 when I was sweet on Al and when we were courting. Not easy to love a seminarian. He left the Paulist Brothers in Baltimore to marry me. His mother pushed him to be a priest. You have no idea what a vamp I was! I went down to DC to visit Cousin Elsie and Aunt Katherine, and we took him out to dinner, but I never kept him from doing what he wanted to do. We married after the war, and then he enlisted in the Air Force."

Letter to My Adoptive Father

Dear Dad,

Long after your death, I write these thoughts I could never share with you. I could never tell you what was important to me. That I write them at all is proof that you gave me a good life. I don't need to sell myself on the benefits to my young life with you as my dad. If I question your love, I need only recall how sometimes your sheepish smile made you younger. Your eyes and mouth would soften, and you might chuckle and chide me, pointing out and excusing my naiveté. My foolish little girlishness. You loved me once, I feel sure of it.

The photos Mom took of you holding me when we were still new to each other show how happy and proud you were of me and how I responded with my smiles. Comfortable in your lap at five months, up at your shoulder at eight months, pushed in my stroller—I was happy to be the center of anyone's attention—your pride and joy. In the portraits that followed through my early years, you were settling the record that I was yours. My adoption had sealed it.

Of course, your little girl loved you as you loved her. She revered you. You were her handsome, capable, uniformed hero. You playfully set your dress blue serge officer's cap on her head, and she felt its clumsy weight, the inside brown leather band that held your scent, the two brass eagles that pinned the black strap band at each side, and the E Pluribus Unum of the weighty eagle insignia on the peak above the visor that covered her eyes.

When my personhood began to reveal itself, our differences stood in relief. Did you doubt what you had wished for? When were you first circumspect of me? When did you cast the first sidewise glance? What was the genesis of your anxiety? Was it that you didn't know my origins?

There was so much I wondered about myself. I realize now that you probably didn't know more than the fairy-tale version of how I came to be with you and Mom. The fifties and sixties bound you, a military man, to a postwar protective mindset. Even had you known a smattering more than what the adoption agency suggested you tell me, would you have told me? The secrecy of adoption was firmly in place. You didn't say that my birth mother was "wayward" or "mentally ill" or "morally corrupted," the way church and state cast unwed mothers since Victorian times, but I believe you assumed it. You might have feared her offspring was damaged goods. My birth mother was a ghost who haunted all of us and couldn't speak for herself.

By the time you returned after a year in Thailand, we were disconnected emotionally. We hadn't written to each other. The thread of conversation had snapped. The hard truth is that I felt safer, freer, when you were away. As I write this, I realize that I might have unconsciously wanted to spite you by my transfer to public high, get even for what I saw were your grievances against me.

It is not my intention to carry these grievances so long past your death. I suffered from your unpredict-

able moods, migraines, and intolerance. I wanted to please you. When you returned from temporary duty overseas, no sooner was your blue B-4 bag disembow-eled of its gifts than you returned to harsh disciplinar-ian. You preached, and I listened until I couldn't. I would have loved stories about your childhood that weren't about discipline or danger, about a school where a nun whipped you outside with a rubber hose. Those times—impressed on you—affected me.

You might have thought that to protect me, you had to make me live up—no, perform—to your expec-tations. No child must be expected to pay by their achievements for the gift of their protection. I had to cooperate so you could straighten me out. Fix my character, as if I were your underling, your recruit. If I could tell you this, would you say to me now, "Oh no, we thought nothing of the kind! We loved you unconditionally!" As so many adoptees do, I thought I must be flawed. Otherwise, why would an infant who looks so perfect in your photos be given away? I learned to keep my distance, grew to fear your temper.

You gave and gave, and I accepted with a happy grace, yet I was still disappointed. I became morose when I grew older in the realization of a need you couldn't fill. Now, my heart aches for your bitter loss of the child you didn't have. I am sad for the child who grew up without knowing what became of her family of origin, for the child who struggled to find a place in the family.

In our "permanent home," there were rare happy times when you were relaxed, like on a weekend when you might cook a big pot of homemade bean soup, broil a steak, or cook hamburgers on the round charcoal grill, or on holidays, when the linen table-cloth and good china were laid on the dining room table, your family visited, and you and Nana cooked and served.

I know now nothing is permanent. All of life is transitory. Your military career made our stability as a family virtually impossible. When you saw the changes in me, it must have thrown you, absent so often. You intended to set a firm foundation for me, but I needed more hugs, Dad. Maybe you did too.

In gratitude,
Mary Ellen

Newsprint

The pulpy odor signals his immersion in the *Sunday Times*. In his casual permanent press pants, his legs stretched out, ankles crossed, he studies the first section open on his lap. His relaxed moments are rare. The Sunday ritual is 9:00 a.m. Mass followed by egg-and-bacon breakfast and an afternoon of reverential quiet. Mom and Nana busy themselves with needlework or retreat to their bedrooms. If I risk an inquiry, he might deliver a sermon, so I take a book to the couch, stepping across the papers spread out on the green broadloom. It's prudent to be respectful of his time with his paper.

There might have been interesting topics and opinions to share, but I never heard them in those years. The complexities of what he knew were stricken from the conversation by security. But when Dad retired from government, he was openly conversational. In his later years, he demonstrated this authority and freedom to share and might have sought to instruct, but during the Cold War and Southeast Asian years—the 1960s—his somber features gave me clues about the troubled world he well understood.

~

More about My Dad

Dad made a presentation to Catholic servicemen who were considering careers in Intelligence. Los Angeles (personal archive-undated).

> *"As a member of the parish clergy, I am involved in parochial duties including liturgy, adult education, and chaplain to the hospice of Conejo and persons with AIDS. But my most active work is among the poor and homeless of Los Angeles. For the majority of my adult life, I served in the U.S. government as an operational Intelligence officer. For over 24 years I was in Intelligence in the United States Air Force, and for nearly 14 years I was employed by the Central Intelligence Agency, the last six years of which I was Chief for the Los Angeles field office, covering a large area of [sic] Southwest United States. As an Intelligence Operations officer, I was involved in aerial reconnaissance, aircrew briefings, prison camp survival, escape, and evasion, prisoner interrogation, agent training, and handling and collection of foreign intelligence information.*
>
> *Often I have been asked if there was any contradiction between my service in intelligence and my role*

in the clergy as a permanent deacon. Unequivocally, I have said that there is never a conflict. Never in 38 years of intelligence work, was I ever ordered or volunteered to do anything immoral or unethical. Many times I have discussed this question with my confessor and spiritual advisers, and never have I received a negative response. As a matter of fact, when I applied for and was called to be a permanent deacon, I went through several personal interviews with priests, psychiatrists, and personality tests, and never once was there any problem. Peter Garrity, retired Archbishop of Newark, New Jersey, who ordained me in 1977, and the late Cardinal Timothy Manning of Los Angeles never were concerned with my dual status. I have a strong faith in God and a deep love of country.

My spiritual life has been great. For most of my life, wherever I have been, I have managed to attend daily Mass, with very few exceptions. I say the Rosary or my Office of the Hours on a regular basis, and wherever possible I have had the grace of regular retreats, even when I was in the Air Force...

The Intelligence career is filled with many great personal opportunities for an individual. I began as an infantryman—a so-called grunt, GI Joe—in World War II, rose through the enlisted ranks, and received a direct field commission as an officer. I received education in photography, photogrammetry, and leadership. Between World War II and 1950, I received a college degree from a Catholic university under the GI Bill of Rights.

I was recalled to the Air Force for the Korean Conflict, in which I served as an Aerial Reconnaissance officer, and Associate Professor of Air Science, and an Aide to the NATO Command. [Iceland] Meanwhile, my education continued. I took 12 hours of Theology at Fordham University and graduated from Air Command and Staff College in 1956 and 1957. The Air Force sent me to Columbia University for a master's degree in Economic Geography. I served for short tours on an aircraft carrier, and in a submarine for cross-training with the Navy. I attended the Strategic Intelligence and Research Program at Brookings Institute and Johns Hopkins University School of Advanced International Studies, and Seton Hall University's Far East Studies Division, and the State Department Foreign Service Institute.

I recount all of this because I want you to see my training was mostly academic. I do not recall ever training on weapons, bombs, poisons, or any of the nefarious instruments seen on Mission Impossible or James Bond movies. Intelligence is a good, challenging, and rewarding career. The pay is good, the opportunities exist for a rewarding occupation. I have had a lot of satisfaction, and enjoy my substantial retirement benefits. Much of my experience and my benefits enable me to devote full time to a diocesan role as a deacon in service to God's people."

Snapshot of the Era and My Father's Military Service

1951–12/1952 Shaw AFB SC—Reconnaissance Squad—adoption 10/52–Maxwell AFB, Alabama training in ROTC instruction

19/53–1954 Athens, OH, ROTC instructor and courses at Maxwell

6/1/1954–11/1/1955 Saigon military mission in South Vietnam under US Air Force Col. Edward Lansdale, Vietnam War begins

1955 New Jersey home built

1955—1956 Iceland NATO command

9/1956–5/1957 Kindergarten

9/1957-1958 First grade, Victoria, TX, Dad assigned to Tokyo

1958–1961 Second grade–mid fourth grade—2 schools. England AFB Louisiana—UFO Ops.

1959 Cuba—Batista overthrown, Castro assumes power

1/20/1961 Kennedy inauguration, Russia and US rhetoric over "Missile Gap"

1/1961 Second half of fourth grade, NJ

4/17–4/20/1961 Bay of Pigs Invasion

6/1961 Family three-year tour in Tokyo, Dad's many TDYs through Southeast Asia

9/1961—6/1963 Fifth and sixth grades, Sacred Heart, Tokyo

10/11–10/28/1962 Cuban Missile Crisis, US confronts Russian over nuclear warheads

9/1963 Johnson AFB Iruma, Tokyo, seventh grade

11/22/1963 Kennedy Assassination, Dallas, TX, Johnson becomes president

6/64 Report to Langley, VA, Operations, living in NJ, working in NY in Intelligence

1965 USAF bombings of rural Cambodia begin under Johnson

1965–1969—First high school 1965–1967, second 1967–1969

1967–1968 Dad stationed in Northeast Thailand—Intelligence operations

1969—Dad resumes Intelligence work in NYC pending official resignation from USAF

Operation Freedom Deal further expands Cambodia's bombing and continues until August 1973

1969–1974 Nixon Administration

3/18/1969 to 5/26/1970 Operation Menu—covert US bombing campaign in eastern Cambodia, and B-52 carpet bombings under Nixon

1973—Official retirement as Lt. Col. and stays with CIA

4/30/1975 Fall of Saigon, end of Vietnam War

Arlington

Rows of white folding chairs on the lawn accommodated all that remained of his family and East Coast colleagues. It had been years since my father and I connected at any depth. When he sold our New Jersey home, my foundation in 1975, my heart, once again, was lost. It was his heart in the end. He'd survived bypass surgeries.

Mom told me not to travel west for his funeral the summer of 1999. The well-attended ceremony for a retired Air Force, Central Intelligence officer, and permanent deacon was held in the affluent parish where he served. "I'll see you at Arlington." She brought the booklet and biography he had penned in anticipation of the inevitable.

I was forty-eight when I approached my adoptive father's graveside and looked down our years of estrangement. His high standards, his anger, and his absences: I weighed these recollections against my need for acceptance, my sensitivity, and my rebelliousness.

As the caisson passed, I held Mom's hand. A stoic, devoted, dutiful officer's wife once again stayed behind. She knew the sting of separation and felt her share of resentment. She had cried privately over the past weeks and months. My tears of lost affection, forgiveness, and regret wouldn't flow—for now. The salute was fired for soldiers felled by age and infirmity or carried home from foreign fields.

My Returns to Mother

I maneuvered her wheelchair up to the chunky, square table near the wide window of her room. When I last visited her in May, I covered it with a loosely woven green cloth. I arranged framed photos, her magenta glass vase with a bunch of bright, life-like daffodils, and her lamp painted with a songbird in a Japanese cherry tree.

The photos: Mom with her then-young parents at her graduation. She had just received her bachelor of science in nursing at St. John's University in New York City. A picture with my Dad in the eighties. A portrait of Nana in her garden when she was close to Mom's age, and my daughter's boys at ages five and ten. They lived in Chicago, and she hadn't seen them for six years before she came here. She rarely seemed comfortable in assisted living, although she was no longer able to manage her life in her small nearby home. Now in nursing care, she seemed more resigned.

A gold-papered cardboard stationery box in her bottom dresser drawer held antique photos. Sitting beside her, I bent to my right to open it, retrieve the box, and place it in front of her. Only a few words were needed to direct the simple activity we had repeated many times. I lifted the lid and took out half the stack of photos. She held the black-and-white images more closely to her face each time we did this, and she struggled to name the blurry figures. She described what she could see of the faded scenes from farm and city—long-lost friends, places, memories from close to a century ago.

Mom's paternal grandparents immigrated to Ellis Island from Austria-Hungary, at the turn of the twentieth century, to a homestead in central Pennsylvania where they built a palatial log home, raised many children, and worked a dairy farm. In a studio portrait taken several years before her birth in 1922, their brood of fourteen stood in rows, wearing their Sunday best, the proud Momma and Papa seated at the front. My mother pointed to Michael, her dad, but couldn't identify the babe in arms or the two children at their mother's knee. Each year, the young women and men—aunts and uncles she spent time with as a girl—became less familiar to her.

Today Mom is sociable and lucid, so we chat over wonderful black-and-whites her mother took of her: a little girl in a plain dress standing in a flower patch or on a dirt road with her little friends or a rustic Pennsylvania porch. In 1929, her parents drove away from the farm and coal country with Mary Agnes when she finished first grade at the one-room schoolhouse. They left behind her younger brother, Vincent, to stay with his grandparents and uncles on the Tokar dairy farm until they could find work in the city.

Mom slumps on a sweltering Lower East Side stoop. She poses next on a tenement rooftop with Vincent and a scraggly dog, whose name she says is Carlo. She softly exclaims at one in which she is framed by Washington Square Park's Triumphal Arch. Right hand on her hip, the seven-year-old Agnes wears a shirtwaist and Mary Janes, and she squints at her mother's camera under Buster Brown bangs. Her only doll is plaster and jointed, a gift from the wife of her father's new employer, wearing a gold velour coat and white, fur-trimmed hat.

My mother reveals fragments of a sentimental story in which she longs for her rustic birthplace. Within that peaceful place in her memory reside her parents, aunts, and uncles. Especially Momma. Any memory of her family's servile work for diminishing returns has faded. There is no hunger, want, or illness in her dream. No sadness. I know a place like that in my bones: the Scots, Irish, and Welsh heritage I learned of through a DNA test.

Emotions swirl through the stale sensations of her room. The conditioned air is chilled despite my good intentions, my attempts to engage a woman who never easily made connections with me. I'm one of few left in her life, yet after sixty-seven years, she finds it hard to reach out to me and asks nothing of the one who wants to help, giving her all I can. Were my mother's wary, suspicious nature and unattractive traits of jealousy passed on to her along with her ready laughter, her handiwork talent, and strength? She says she didn't know or understand me but stops short of expressing her regret for mothering a child not her own by birth.

I sit by her as she dozes in the recliner and study her face, her occasional winces and eye twitches. Restless, I check my cell phone and then rise with my cane. For eleven years, I've struggled with the weakness and uncertain balance caused by a stroke. I walk to her closet to adjust her clothes and then fuss with her dresser items, a basket of hairbands, mini hand lotions, a tiny ceramic vase of dried flowers, and a clay infant Jesus statue she's had since childhood, his two raised fingers snapped off long ago. Pine trees sway outside the closed windows while she rests in dim light, in the solitary space of the very old where I risk intrusion.

She's vulnerable and knows I see she is, which makes it harder for us. When Dad died fifteen years ago, I sold their house of twenty-seven years and made a home for her in Pennsylvania. I stood by her through her mother's death, household care, and transition to assisted living, and I supported her healthcare decisions. I see the weak link in her trust, her resentment. The nursing staff assures me she doesn't mean it when she says, "You're not my real daughter" or tells me to get out. "I don't want you here!" I no longer retort when she rages unfiltered at me. I walk away.

I should stop the unsolicited help. It makes her uneasy, and I exhaust myself when I try too much. We're reminded of our family connection when I bring her necessities and a few luxuries. Except for the Life Savers she craves, she doesn't look for anything from me. My husband and I make frequent trips to and from Florida to allow me time with her. I know I am the one who clings. It is my need to attach, my need to nurture. I walk the line between my needs and hers and cross it when she remembers I am not hers, when I remind her of a child she and her husband couldn't have.

In October 2019, at ninety-seven, she knows that she is in end-of-life care. Each in our way, we struggle with the shortness of time. She tries to separate from me, from the earth. I have felt separation since birth. She, the mother who raised me, felt the sting of loneliness each time my father was away. That was how military life was. All the while, I struggled with an unexplained sense of loss.

My adoptive mother, Agnes, passed away in June 2020 at nine-eight. It hurt me, and perhaps her as well, that we could not be together. Her nursing facility was closed because of COVID-19. I'm thankful that she knew me on our last Zoom call, and that I recorded her wrinkled, authentic smile, and her motherly voice.

Abandonment

in the nursing home
my very old mother says:
"Don't forget to call
Don't forget I'm here."

I have learned the wound of relinquishment
means that
the feeling you are left behind never stops

Never stop loving me. Don't leave me behind.
Take me with you.

Part Twenty-One

River Songs

I am three going on four. I linger where our patchy new lawn stops and the sandy soil starts, and then I venture into the rutted ground. I explore the scrubby habitat of all that crawls, creeps, and leaps—insects of childhood—black beetles, prickly caterpillars, roly polies, katydids, and ladybugs. The barren plot beside our new home is filled with more than grown-ups realize. I'm happy to be topless in plaid shorts. My mother brushes my light-brown hair and braids the top and sides back into two bows. My loose curls lie gently on my skin. With my pink plastic scissors, I snip seed heads of tall grasses that tickle my legs, and I claim this wild place as my empty lot.

The old field with oaks, maples, and birch saplings is my refuge. I am far enough from McCree's red barn and clapboard house, from five-year-old Ben's taunts. Beyond the wire-looped fence, I hear Nana's plain melodies as she works among her roses and keeps me in her watchful eye.

I sing fragments of Nana's songs in the old Czech dialect, songs from my stack of Golden Records, and the popular songs I hear on our kitchen countertop Stromberg-Carlson. At four, music comes from my heart like a river swell.

"Every second of the minute, every minute of the hour, every hour of the day, I love you." I sing without knowing what I know—that I am loved. I twirl to the scratchy rhythm of crickets, spin barefooted until I fall, giddy in a heap of happiness.

Lenni Lenape, the original people of New Jersey, the peaceful hunter-gatherers, camped along the Hackensack River. In the spring, mothers and children sang while they planted their gardens, wove grass mats, and cooked meals over coals. Fathers hunted with flint arrowheads, their voices raised in song while they crafted tools of stone, wood, and bone. These gentle, nomadic people canoed far downstream to spend summer along the beaches, cool themselves in saltwater, and gather and feast on oysters, clams, and wild plums. When they returned upstream, they harvested their fall gardens, wild grapes, and berries and fished in the crystal freshwater river. Clans hunkered, warmed within their wigwams by fires vented to the stars. The forest provided plenty of deer, small mammals, and fowl, and the people subsisted on dried corn, beans, and squash.

Sparrows sip rainwater that puddles in white birch clumps. The black-etched trees with fragrant, peeling bark, drop green, wiggly catkins that I cook in my tiny tin pot for dolly. When they are ripe and brown, I crumble them, and they scatter like dandelion fluff in the breeze. My lips and fingers are stained by black raspberries. A brown rabbit shelters until dusk in her warren beneath the thorny thicket. Mice skitter, their tracks alive with curiosity.

In time, Nana's flowers need me to water them, and there are weeds to pull. There are ballet lessons in my black leotard and kindergarten to make friends. My parents didn't think our moves mattered to me. Children were resilient and adaptable, they might have thought. Because I had lost my first mother and was moved again before these parents took me with them, I now believe it mattered. I want to stay with Nana in our home. Feelings tell me that people and places are missing. Even so, the moves and changes engender memories, stories to tell, and my stories must complete me.

In our green Buick Special, we cross the Old Bridge in River Edge to shop in Hackensack. From the bridge, I have seen families splash in bathing suits at the sandy Steuben Landing. I've seen them fish from motorboats.

~

David Demarest, a Huguenot, obtained a patent from France for land along the Hackensack River, and French Protestants, Dutch, and Swedes settled eight thousand acres west of the Hudson Palisades in 1677. Entrepreneurship and industry flourished along the Hackensack in New Milford's colonial and revolutionary times. The rich river bottom yielded the Jersey farmers' wheat, corn, and buckwheat.

Like the Lenni Lenape, the colonists wove baskets from the hemp they harvested from the woodlands. The indigenous people fashioned the red riverbed clay into pots and vessels to trade with the colonists, who described them as the placid "Unami, people of the upriver." The Lenni Lenape tried to coexist with them but weren't immune to their cruel treatment or illnesses and alcohol.

~

Dear child, you learned many were not yours, and not many were your own. You came from somewhere else, but when the curtain was behind you, you were fitting in. You came on the scene like a special star. You knew the smiles, the steps, the songs. They praised you and smiled, and that kept you smiling.

In those days, you learned you were not the same, and you told the children on the playground you were not like them. You weren't comfortable that you were different but couldn't say why. The causes were distorted. The reasons weren't clear, and there were times when you were not okay.

Why would the one who was above you hurt a girl like you? Why would he make those marks as he learned from his long-dead father? You had to get away when the yelling wouldn't stop, when the tears were bitter and salty and your gasps wouldn't let up. You were special, and you wouldn't be like the others. Who were you, anyway? You were not his, but you were under him. You'd be better, best, if he had to beat it into you. You could be someone.

~

A Dutch settler, Jan Zabriskie, built a grist mill in 1714 at Steuben Landing and a dam to form a pond to run his waterwheel at high tide. Flour brought a higher price to farmers who brought him grain. In 1744, a sliding draw bridge, New Bridge, was built. It was the first crossing above Newark Bay. General Washington made Zabriskie's home his headquarters in 1780. After the war, Zabriskie returned to his home, and the mill and store proved vibrant. Heavy sloops carried local products and iron ore from the mountains of northern Jersey down to Newark Bay.

~

Scots-Irish from Ulster and Germans from the Palatinate sailed away from persecution and war. Quakers and Presbyterians settled near the Philadelphia port, some in Chester and Delaware Counties. They drove covered wagons pulled by oxen southwest into Maryland on the Native American trail called the Great Warrior Path. These rugged pioneers named this main route the Conestoga wagon trail—the Great Valley Road that runs out to Central Pennsylvania, down the Appalachians through Virginia, the Blue Ridge, and through the North Carolina backcountry. Through Indian wars and revolution, many trekked into South Carolina. My ancestors farmed south of the new city of Greenville in the fertile Fork Shoals at the confluence of Huff Creek and the Reedy River. These rocky shoals were well used by the Cherokee people and the early pioneers. The old mill at Fork Shoals, powered by the strong current, began operation in 1870. My ancestors called the place Grove.

At the airport, Leila Cox stood with her walker, refusing the wheelchair, her leg prosthesis be damned, and it touched my heart. Her visible imperfections didn't matter to me. She was powerful. Despite her failings, she showed her beauty, her natural, down-to-earth demeanor, and her spunk. She was my mother, the woman who gave me life. I was relieved of the burden of wanting, the need to know. The euphoria of our fall reunion arose like a phoenix from years of pain and loss.

Leila Cox had curiosity, but our fate was sealed when she signed me away under the state's promise that she should not hope to see me again. We were alike in our brown hair and eyes, our tone of voice, the lilt and wit that hid a quieter, darker sadness. We were alike in temperament and a smidge of Cherokee cheekbones. In the longing in our hearts.

I'd heard the range of her high, strong voice that sprang from poor South Carolina mothers, the songs that had come to me on the radio waves, the honky-tonk, and the gospel songs she sang in church. I felt the hearty laughter that rocked her. From within her womb, I felt her riled emotions, the clutch of her heavy sobs, grip of her fear, her anger, her dread, her restlessness. I heard her voice that waited on servicemen in Greenville and Charleston bars. Like the voices of carders and bobbin winders on the Reedy River—the Conestee, Poe, Pendleton, Monaghan textile mills—poor women who lived in shabby saltbox shanties with their millworker daddies. Mothers who lived in mill villages along rail tracks near the waterfalls. Their heritage, the Scots-Irish voyagers, pilgrims, farmers, soldiers, mothers, fathers, musicians, and weavers. Their tales, stories, and myths, their lies and secrets.

In Greenville, with the guidance of search angels, gene-alogists, and my newly found family, I discovered my ancestors' gravestones in Antioch, Standing Springs, and Rocky Creek churchyards. Cousin Lawrence gave me a formal photograph—a portrait—made in 1916 of his grandparents: my great-grandparents, Mary Henriette Lenderman, and John Quincey Cox. At sixty-two, Mary is wearing a long, black wool cape suit with a high-collared white blouse—the winter garb of a prominent farmer's wife. Her brown hair is parted at the center and pinned up, her gaze is steadfast, serene, and dignified, her cheekbones high and proud. She stands next to her husband, her left hand resting on his right shoulder. Her fingers are long like mine. John is graying and mustached, aging from their hard farming life.

My half-sister, Karen, had honored Mary Henriette at the Antioch Church Cox-Lenderman reunion on October

15, 1997, years before our own reunion:

She was born near here in the Saint Alburn commu-
nity and attended school there. Her education was
very limited—only fifth or sixth grade—which was not
unusual at that time. Her mother, Tabitha, died when
Mary was nine, at thirty-one years old. Her father,
William, married her mother's sister when her mother
died. Mary married John Quincy Cox and bore at
least eleven children of whom we are the descendants.

A tall woman with long black hair; perhaps this is
where a lot of us got our height. She lived in a time when
women had but little say-so in their homes and were
expected to have large families and stay in the home.

She was known as a hard-working woman, taking
care of her home and garden. John and Mary farmed
seventy acres near this church in a place called Grove.
Dawn to dusk work with no modern conveniences.
She washed clothes in tubs with a scrub board.

She canned food to sustain them through the
winter. I have been told that she was a good cook and
baked great apple pies, blackberry pies, and biscuits, all
done on a wood stove. She was active in the church. She
treated all her children alike and was a good mother
not only to her kids but also to her grandchildren.

She survived her husband by four years and died
November 5, 1928, after an illness of seven months.
She wasn't famous, never drove a car or voted, or went
very far from her home, but she should be remem-
bered as a great lady who molded a lot of lives.

Mary Ellen Gambutti

My birth mother told me, "I wondered about you. I hoped you'd have a good life. I wanted the nuns to give you a good home." Over the next year, I continued to return to Greenville and saw her health decline. I'd learned about her parents' poverty and the unsettled life they passed on to her, lack of education and low self-esteem, her increasing ill health, bouts of "nerves" when her mind would "go blank," and her "spells," when her thoughts would "whirl" and she "couldn't think." Was there a neurological connection to my history of panic, sensory episodes, and catastrophic thoughts? Were they caused by the separation that harmed us both? Her brother Wilton, who had severe epilepsy and a mental disorder; her daughter Susan's epilepsy; and her sister, Annie, I suspect a hereditary link. Are these traits passed to me?

Leila died at sixty-nine, the age I am at this writing. Karen and I were among the few at her funeral. Her legacy was more than a closet of ordinary clothes, a few pieces of costume jewelry, cards and letters we'd exchanged, and her lifetime of regrets and foggy memories.

I hope she thought I proved the need to know her, and although abbreviated, our time together was meaningful—that I am part of her legacy. I hope that I have done right by her.

～

Long before I played there, my empty lot lay in a Hackensack riverbed. A summer gust that blew grit into my eye etched the earth for a brown sparrow's dust bath. Redbirds and robins sang songs for me, and I sang for them.

～

*My maternal great grandparents,
Mary and John Cox.*

AFTERWORD

In 1990, when I tentatively began my search journey, I was unaware of an *Adoption Reform Movement*; that Florence Fisher was the founder of *Adoptees' Liberty Movement Association (ALMA)*. I hadn't heard of Jean Paton's struggles and *Orphan Journey*. I didn't realize that the seeds of adoptee search in the United States had long before blossomed, and that the *American Adoption Congress* existed to unify the burgeoning number of search and support groups in the 1970s. I was unaware that so many others were driven to search their birth mothers—that there was such an innate need. I didn't know that American adoptees were fighting for their original birth certificates, were foiled and persisted, and that archaic, restrictive domestic adoption laws must change. I continue to learn from my adoptee peers and advocates. My efforts to reach out to my family of origin were rewarded far beyond some vague notion to identify the woman who gave me life. I succeeded because of the strength and assistance of those who came before me.

I have not touched on intercountry adoption, but as I have begun to read adoptees' stories, I gain a sense of the complexity and injustice rife in the lives of international adoptees. I include a note here from my friend, Ande Stanley, an international adoptee:

International adoptees face many obstacles in pursuit of our adoption documents, proof of citizenship, and passports. There are barriers to access such as foreign language, unfamiliar bureaucratic requirements, and a complete non-uniformity of law regarding adoption across countries, and the dismal reality of child trafficking. The demand for children far exceeds the supply. Yes. We are a commodity. Our human rights are violated as we are cut off from our cultures, languages, and families by law, time, and distance.

In my case, I was fortunate that the United Kingdom has a process in place for adoptees seeking their files. The process still took me two years to complete and cost me considerably more than a non-adoptee would pay for their birth information. A copy of my mothers' original birth certificate cost me two dollars and a stamp. I had spent hundreds of dollars by the time mine arrived."

—Ande Stanley was born in England and came to the United States with her adoptive father and mother. Her father served in the USAF as an officer and physician. She blogs at The Adoption Files. https://theadoptionfiles.com.wordpress.com/blog

NOTES

"6 Reasons Not to Give I.Q. Tests to Young Children," Lisa Van Gemert, https://www.giftedguru.com/6-reasons-not-to-give-iq-tests-to-young-children/.

"About Jean Paton & This Book: The Biography of Jean Paton the Mother of the Adoption Reform Movement," E. Wayne Carp, https://jeanpaton.com/about-e-wayne-carp.

"Adopted Child Living in Fear," Adoptee Blogspot (link no longer available).

"Baptismal Certificate in Adoption," http://www.vatican.va.

"Ghosts in the Adopted Family," *Psychoanalytic Inquiry*, Betty Jean Lifton, https://pacer-adoption.org/wp-content/uploads/2014/03/47240532.pdf.

"How Does a CIA Operative Become a Charity Ringleader," Victoria Giraud, October 31, 2008, https://www.latimes.com/archives/la-xpm-1998-jan-12-me-7557-story.html.

"Is Catholic Adoption Different Than Regular Adoption," Gladney Center for Adoption, November 16, 2020, https://adoption.org/is-catholic-adoption-different-than-regular-adoption.

"Study of the Treatment of Juvenile Delinquency in Ohio," Ashley H. Weeks, Educational Research Bulletin, https://www.jstor.org/stable/1473866.

"The Psychology of the Adopted Child," Florence Clothier, The Adoption History Project, http://www.uoregon.edu.

"The Oratory: Seventy-Five Years of Abiding Faith," Jennifer Becknell, The Herald, February 10, 2008, https://www.heraldonline.com/living/article12208619.html.

ADOPTEE RESOURCES

Adoptee Rights Campaign, Intercountry Adoptee Citizenship, Adoptee Rights Campaign–News and Information, https://adopteerightscampaign.org.

Adoptee Rights Coalition, https://www.adopteerightscoalition.com, "Dedicated to changing unjust laws and archaic policies and practices rooted in stigma, shame, and secrecy by restoring unfettered access to original birth certificates and adoption records for adult adoptees."

Adoptees Connect, https://www adopteesconnect.com, "Peer-led adoptee centric support for adult adoptees."

Adoptees On, Haley Radke, https://www.adopteeson.com, "A gathering of incredible adopted people willing to share their intimately personal stories with you about the impact adoption has had on our lives. Listen in and you will discover that you are not alone on this journey."

This Adoptee Life, Amanda Medina, https://www.facebook.com/thisadopteelife/?ti=as.

Adoptees Unite, A National Adoptee Rights Organization, https://adopteesunited.org/positions.

The Adoption Files, Ande Stanley, https://theadoptionfile-scom.wordpress.com/blog. "A place to talk about the emotional and physical side of accessing our identities."

The Adoption History Project: Bastard Nation, https://pages.uoregon.edu/adoption/people/bastardnation.htm.-consent

Adoption: My Truth, Laureen Pittman, https://adoptionmy-truth.com/about/.

Akin to the Truth: A Memoir of Adoption and Identity, Paige Strickland, https://stricklandp.wordpress.com.

The ALMA Society, https://www.almasociety.org. "The original pioneer nonprofit organization fighting for the rights of adoptees everywhere, was founded by adoptee Florence Anna Fisher in 1971…For the past fifty years, our mission is reuniting adoptees and members of their families of origin via our mutual-consent Reunion Registry."

Anne Heffron, https://www.anneheffron.com/blog.

Bastard Nation, the Adoptee Rights Organization, https://www.bastards.org.

Brooke Randolph, https://www.facebook.com/BrookeRandolphLMHC.

——https://www.Brooke-Randolph.com.

——https://www.GreenHouseIndy.com/counseling.

——https://www.instagram.com/BrookeRandolphLMHC.

——https://www.twitter.com/BRandolphLMHC.

Conversations about Adoption, Jen Matthews, https://www.facebook.com/groups/conversationsaboutadoption/?ref=share.

The Declassified Adoptee, Amanda Woolston, http://www.declassifiedadoptee.com.

Diary of a Not So Angry Adoptee, Christina Romo. Korean adoptee and blogger. https://diaryofanotsoangryasian-adoptee.com.

The Family Preservation Project, https://www.familypreservation365.com, https://www.thefamilypreservationpro-ject.com. "It is an interactive site focused on helping expectant and new mothers."

Gregory D. Luce, Interview with Haley Radke, Adoptees On, https://adopteerightslaw.com.

"How Adjusting the Immigration Registry Could Help Inter-country Adoptees–Adoptee Rights Campaign" Inter-country Adoptees, https://intercountryadopteevoices. com/about/vision-mission.

Julie McGue, https://www.juliemcgueauthor.com.

Lavender Luz, Lori Holden, http://lavenderluz.com.

The Lost Daughters, http://www.thelostdaughters.com. "A collaborative writing project featuring the voices of adopted women blogging adoption from a place of empowerment and peace."

My Refocused Life Adopted: A Blog about Adoption, Geneal-ogy, Identity, and Healing, David Brown, https://www. facebook.com/myrefocusedlifeadopted.

No Apologies for Being Me: A Blog about the Adoption Expe-rience, Lynn Grubb, https://noapologiesforbeingme. blogspot.com.

Right to Know, https://righttoknow.us. "Advancing our funda-mental human right to know our genetic identity through education, mental health initiatives, and advocacy."

Saving Our Sisters, https://www.savingoursistersadoption. org. "Supporting expectant mothers to promote family preservation."

Signed, Sealed, Adopted. https://signedsealedadopted.com. Jamie Weiss.

BOOKS

Brodzinky, David, Marshall D. Schechter, and Robin Henig. *Being Adopted: The Lifelong Search for Self.* New York: Anchor Books, 1993.

Carp, E. Wayne. *Jean Paton and the Struggle to Reform American Adoption.* Ann Arbor: University of Michigan Press, 2014.

Fessler, Ann. *The Girls Who Went Away: The Hidden History of Women Who Surrendered Children for Adoption in the Decades Before Roe v. Wade.* New York: Penguin, 2006.

Gediman, Judith S., and Linda P. Brown. *Birth Bond: Reunions between Birthparents and Adoptees—What Happens After.* Far Hills, NJ: New Horizon Press,1991.

Gilbert, Suzanne, Reunion Land Bookshelves: Adoptees, DCPs & Fostereds, https://bookshop.org/shop/reunion-landpress.

Grubb, Lynn, ed. *The Adoptee Survival Guide: Adoptees Share Their Wisdom and Tools.* CreateSpace Independent Publishing Platform, 2015.

Heffron, Anne. *You Don't Look Adopted.* New York: Running Water Press, 2016.

Lifton, Betty Jean. *Journey of the Adopted Self: A Quest for Wholeness.* Basic Books, 1995.

———. *Lost and Found: The Adoption Experience.* New York:The Dial Press, 1983.

———. *Twice Born: Memoirs of an Adopted Daughter.* New York: Other Press, 2006.

McGue, Julie Ryan. *Twice a Daughter: A Search for Identity, Family, and Belonging.* Berkley: She Writes Press, 2021.

Pickell, Karen. *An Adoptee Lexicon.* Clearwater: Raised Voice Press, 2018.

Pittman, Laureen. *The Lies That Bind: An Adoptee's Journey Through Rejection, Redirection, DNA, and Discovery.* Independently published, 2019.

Randolph, Brooke, ed. *It's Not About You: Understanding Adoptee Search, Reunion, and Open Adoption.* Ann Arbor: Entourage Publishing, 2017.

———. "Red Flags That a Therapist Could Do More Harm Than Good." In *Adoption Therapy: Perspectives from Clients and Clinicians on Processing and Healing Post-Adoption Issues,* edited by Laura Dennis. Redondo Beach: Entourage Publishing, 2014.

———. *The Bully Book: A Workbook for Kids Coping with Bullies.* Ann Arbor: Entourage Publishing, 2016.

———. *The Choices Book: A Workbook for Kids about Making Choices.* Ann Arbor: Entourage Publishing, 2017.

———. *The Loss Book: A Workbook for Kids Coping with Loss.* Ann Arbor: Entourage Publishing, 2017.

Strickland, Paige Adams. *After the Truth.* Idealized Apps, 2013.

———. *Akin to the Truth: A Memoir of Adoption and Identity.* Idealized Apps, 2017.

van der Kolk, Bessel. *The Body Keeps the Score: Brain, Mind, and Body in the Healing of Trauma.* Reprint edition. New

York: Penguin, 2015.

Verrier, Nancy. *Coming Home to Self: The Adopted Child Grows Up*. Verrier Publishing, 2003.

———. *The Primal Wound: Understanding the Adopted Child*. Baltimore: Newton Gateway Press, 2003.

ACKNOWLEDGMENTS

Great thanks to the editors of the literary magazines who gave first life to the essays; the roots of this book. Basha Krasnoff and Joseph Corrado of *Portland Metrozine,* Dagmara K. of *Spillwords,* Edward King of *A Thousand and One Stories,* Heather of *Wildflower Muse,* Jordan Blum of *Bookends Review,* Elise Matich of *The Remembered Arts Journal,* Monique Berry of *Halcyon Days,* Mary McBeth of *Memoir Magazine,* Sarah Law of *Amethyst Review*, Lisa Shea of *Bella Online,* Based Mountain of *Soft Cartel,* editors of *Drabble Magazine,* Nicole McConnell of *Borrowed Solace,* Ritta M. Basu of *Fewer Than 500,* Nicholas Olsen of *Mac(ro)mic,* Debra Smouse of *Modern Creative Life,* Ray Rasmussen of *Contemporary Haibun Online* and *Haibun Today,* Dave and Jay of *Story Pub,* Janet Kuypers of *CC&D Magazine,* the Editors of *HumanKind Journal,* Amanda of *Gravel Magazine,* Phillip Bannowsky and Steven Leech of *Dreamstreets,* and J. R. Rivero Kinsey of *Blood's Call,* thank you all.

To all the online writing course instructors over these twelve years since my stroke: Sonya Lea helped me to find the words and gave me permission to tell the difficult stories. Jonathan Callard helped me to shape a narrative. Jill Jepson came to the aid of my prose clarity. Robert Vaughn and Meg Tuite of Bending Genres' weekend classes have sparked curiosity and creativity. Sheila Bender's courses and developmental editing have been invaluable. Nellwyn Lampert coached and edited my early book drafts. Thank you, all.

In the adoption community: My dear friend, and a New Jersey adoptee, Noreen, is a supportive reader and ally as we share our stories and new-found ancestries. To the bloggers, genetic genealogists, researchers, authors, and experts in the psychology of adoption who have helped me to clarify, give expression to, and validate my adoptee experience. To the angels who guided me in my search, shedding light on my path to find my biological mother and kin before internet access: Anne McKuen, Gelee Hendricks, Walter Sheppard, Eileen Longo of Adoption Forum, and Karen Connor of Adoptees & Birthparents in Search.

Research help came from Linda Lee Thompson, and the Search Squad, and Rick Klemetson, when it seemed there was next to nothing to work with. My first-found close match, Sherry, allowed me to mirror her Ancestry.com family tree, enabling me to find paternal kin in Georgia. South Carolina cousins Derrick, Jack, and Nancy led me to my paternal siblings. To Karen, Lottie, Teri, Carol, Libby, and George, much love. For your assistance as I made my journey, I thank you, all.

Many thanks to Patricia Marshall and the stellar team at Luminare Press.

ABOUT THE AUTHOR

Mary Ellen Gambutti's work has been published in many literary magazines. I Must Have Wandered is her first book published by Luminare Press. Her previously published books are Stroke Story: My Journey There and Back, Coming to Terms: My Journey Continues, and Permanent Home.

Connect with Mary Ellen Gambutti
on social media
https://linktr.ee/SCMel

https://megam-author.com

https://www.linkedin.com/in/mary-ellen-gambutti-author/

https://www.instagram.com/maryelleng.author/

https://www.facebook.com/M.E.Gambutti.Author/

https://twitter.com/melcmg

Thank you for reading. Please write a review
at your place of purchase.